W0374928

NEW YORK 360°

Herausgegeben in Deutschland von
Verlag Karl Müller GmbH
Venloer Str. 1271, 50829 Köln
Tel.: 0049- 0221-13065-0
Fax: 0049- 0221-13065-210

International copyright
© 1994, Priuli & Verlucca, editori / Ivrea (Turin) Italy

Druck: Mai 2002, Mariogros / Turin, Italy

Alle Rechte vorbehalten.
Kein Teil des Werkes darf in irgendeiner Form
(durch Fotokopie, Mikrofilm oder ein ähnliches Verfahren)
ohne die schriftliche Genehmigung des Verlages reproduziert
oder unter Verwendung elektronischer Systeme verarbeitet,
vervielfältigt oder verbreitet werden.

ISBN 3-89893-039-4

NEW YORK 360°

Text / Vittorio Zucconi
Fotos / David Maria Galardi
Zeichnungen / Luisa Romussi / Quid
Historische und Kunstgeschichtliche Recherchen
David Maria Galardi / Maria Luisa Monti

VERLAG KARL MÜLLER

11. September 2001. Alles ist schon gesagt, ist schon geschrieben worden. Ströme von Worten und Tinte, Eindrücke, die in das Kollektivbewusstsein übergegangen sind: ein universelles *Global Village* aus unmenschlich kalten Fernsehbildern, die in einem kurzen Moment die fernsten Gebiete der Erde erreichten. Nach diesem schrecklichen Morgen, nach diesen zwei titanischen Einstürzen, die die reine, makellose Geometrie der Twin Towers zerstört und zu viele wehrlose Opfer gefordert haben, hat Amerika sich geändert. Unsere Welt hat sich geändert – wir haben diese Wende schon vor Augen – und die Nachwirkung dieser Flut von Hass und Gewalt wird unser aller Leben noch für lange Zeit belasten. New York hat eine klaffende Wunde erlitten – eine Wunde, die bis wenige Sekunden vor den zwei surrealen, entsetzlichen Flammenangriffen gegen den kalten, sterilen Glanz dieser Kristall- und Stahlkolosse undenkbar gewesen war. New York hat sich geändert, hat in einem einzigen Augenblick das leuchtende Symbol nicht nur der Metropole, sondern einer ganzen Lebensauffassung verloren. Die Giganten des World Trade Centers waren kaum mehr als zwanzig Jahre alt, aber es ist, als sei uns das Kolosseum genommen worden, der Eiffelturm oder Big Ben. Doch das Bild dieser Zwillingstürme wird für immer in unserem Gedächtnis bleiben. Ground Zero wird wieder zugeschüttet werden, die gezackte Skyline des «Big Apple» wird uns bald – dessen sind wir sicher – mit einem neuen, überwältigenden technologischen Wunder überraschen, mit einem vielleicht sogar noch höheren und stolzer gegen den Himmel aufragenden Bauwerk. Aber diese zwei perfekten Formen werden wir niemals vergessen – wie wir niemals den sinnlosen Tod so vieler Unschuldiger aus unserem Gedächtnis verdrängen werden. So kommt diesem Buch, das schon gleich nach Erscheinen ein großer Erfolg war, jetzt aber in seinen Bildern und Texten zwangsläufig überholt ist, heute ein neuer Wert, eine andere Bedeutung zu: Es wird zu einem wertvollen Dokument und einem Instrument, um nicht zu vergessen.

Der Verleger

11 September 2001: the tale has been told in its entirety. Torrents of words, both spoken and written, a flood of horrifying pictures, have etched their message on the collective memory of our global village, whose single heart was wrenched by the scenes so coldly and pitilessly thrown across the TV screens of even the world's remotest quarters. Since that accursed morning, since the titanic onslaughts that scythed the neat geometry of the Twin Towers and so many defenceless lives, America has changed. Our world will no longer be the same – the difference is already all too plain. The long wave of this obscure tsunani of hate and violence will muddy our lives for many a year to come. The deep wound that gashed New York was beyond the reach of human imagination until a few seconds before those appalling bursts of flame sprang out against the shining splendour of the two colossal columns of glass and steel. New York orphaned of what were the sparkling symbols not only of a metropolis, but of the world at large, will never be the same. The giants of the World Trade Center had not long come of age, yet their loss cuts as deep as if Rome, France or London had been shorn of its Colosseum, Eiffel Tower or Big Ben. Their image will abide untarnished in our memory. The awesome «Ground Zero» chasm will be filled. The jagged skyline of the Great Apple will once again astonish us. Some other technological marvel will arise, perhaps even taller, and claw the sky with even greater pride. Those two perfect forms, however, will not be forgotten, nor will memory lose sight of the senseless massacre of so many innocent lives. This book, therefore, a success when it first appeared and now perforce the bearer of «dated» photos and texts, has acquired a new worth, a different meaning. It has become a document, a reminder of such much to remember.

The Publisher

Text

Vittorio Zucconi

War es die Augusthitze, die nach zergehendem Asphalt roch, nach Feuchtigkeit, Dunst und Menschen? Oder war es die Müdigkeit nach einer nicht enden wollenden Reise, mit den üblichen sommerlichen Verspätungen und den langwierigen Zollkontrollen («Was versteckst du da im Koffer, Italiener: Salami? Mortadella? Würste?»)? Der erste Eindruck, den ich von New York habe, als ich hier vor über zwanzig Jahren ankam, kann mit einem einzigen Begriff beschrieben werden: Schwindel. Ein Gefühl wie bei dem Blick aus dem Grund eines Canyons heraus, von unten nach oben. Der verwirrende Klang der unterschiedlichsten Sprachen und Akzente, die alle zusammen gesprochen und geschrien wurden. Schwindel bei der Betrachtung der Architektur: Harte, senkrechte und waagerechte Linien, ohne die sanften barocken oder klassizistischen Rundungen der europäischen Städte. Das «déjà vu» einer unbekannten Stadt aus einem regelmäßig wiederkehrenden Traum, der jetzt plötzlich Wirklichkeit wird und dich angreift.

Jahrzehnte sind vergangen seit meiner ersten Nacht in New York, die ich schlaflos im Zimmer eines billigen Hotels verbrachte, während ich auf das Türschloss starrte, das offensichtlich schon mehrmals aufgebrochen worden war. Aber dieses Schwindelgefühl bin ich bis heute nicht losgeworden, ja, ich bin überzeugt, dass ich es niemals verliere. Ich habe das New York der Armen und das der Reichen kennen gelernt. Ich habe in «Le Cirque», dem teuersten Lokal von ganz Manhattan, zu Abend gegessen und Hot Dogs mit Senf an den Würstchenbuden der Afghanen und Äthiopier verzehrt. Ich habe die Museen bewundert und bin durch die Bronx gegangen. Ich bin auf der Straße überfallen worden und habe Woody Allen übelsten Jazz spielen hören. Ich habe in Luxushotels und in «Lofts» meiner Freunde übernachtet. Und ich kenne New York heute weniger als damals, als ich zum ersten Mal herkam; denn diese Stadt verändert sich ununterbrochen. Deshalb kann man sie niemals wirklich kennen lernen. Man kann sie nur (er)leben.

Ich habe mich an dieses Schwindelgefühl gewöhnt wie ein Trinker an die Flasche oder ein Spieler an die Roulettekugel. Ich weiss, dass es mir nicht gut tut, dass ich nicht trinken oder spielen dürfte, aber ich kann nicht ohne auskommen. Die Emotionen, die die anderen Städte der Welt in mir hervorrufen, sind im Vergleich dazu farblos und fade, wie lauwarmes, abgestandenes Bier. Tokio ist größer, aber es ist ein anonymer, geordneter Ameisenhaufen, der keinen Schwindel erregt. Paris ist schöner, aber distanzierter, ist in jedem seiner Steine französisch-arrogant. Rom ist rührend und melancholisch wie eine heruntergekommene Adelige, die den Tee in abgenutzten Tassen aus feinstem Porzellan serviert. London ist das Denkmal einer für immer toten Vergangenheit, ist großartig und nunmehr nutzlos.

New York dagegen sind wir. New York gehört allen. Es gibt kein Volk auf der Erde, das nicht ein Stück New York für sich beanspruchen könnte. Die Afrikaner besitzen hier die größte schwarze Gemeinschaft außerhalb des afrikanischen Kontinents: 2,1 Millionen dunkelhäutige Menschen, die vor allem jenseits des Flusses Harlem leben, nördlich von Manhattan. Italien und China haben hier Städte in Städten errichtet. Hier gibt es mehr Juden als in allen anderen Teilen der Welt. Hier gibt es mehr äthiopische Restaurants als im ganzen, armen Äthiopien. Hier gibt es mehr Puertoricaner als in San Juan di Puerto Rico. Hier gibt es ein «Klein-Russland», ein «Klein-Dublin», ein «Klein-Saigon», ein «Klein-Warschau», ein «Klein-Manila».

In Paris muss man Französisch können, in Rom Italienisch, in Tokio Japanisch. In New York kann man ein ganzes Leben leben, ohne ein einziges Wort Englisch zu sprechen. Hier findest du immer eine Hebamme, einen Arzt, einen Beamten, einen Totengräber, der deine Sprache oder deinen Dialekt spricht, der dich zur Welt bringt, dich traut und dich begräbt, auch wenn du Mandarin oder Kurdisch sprichst. Die Stadt lässt sich ohne Gegenwehr und ungerührt vom ältesten ihrer Einwohner in Besitz nehmen wie vom jüngsten, vom Milliardär wie vom illegalen Einwanderer. Es gibt auf der Welt keinen anderen Ort, an dem man sich so leicht verstecken und so gut untertauchen kann. Wer ungesetzliche Wege beschreiten will, geht nach New York, wo das Verbrechen sich lohnt: Nur eines von zehn Delikten wird bestraft. Nur bei einem von dreißig Raubüberfällen wird der Schuldige verurteilt. Seit einigen Jahren ist New York nicht einmal mehr eine weiße Stadt. Die Bevölkerung europäischer

Abstammung ist nunmehr in der Minderheit, stellt nur noch 43% der 7.322.564 Personen dar, die die fünf «boroughs» bewohnen, die fünf Stadtteile, aus denen New York besteht: Manhattan, Brooklyn, die Bronx, Queens und Staten Island.

Das Schwindelgefühl ist also kein Unwohlsein, sondern die normale, natürliche Verfassung der Menschen hier. Für die einen, die es geschafft haben, die im Rennen um Reichtum, Ruhm und Erfolg als Sieger hervorgegangen sind, ist es der berauschende Sinnestaumel darüber, die schwierigste Stadt der Welt erobert und einen Doktortitel oder einen Oscar des Überlebens gewonnen zu haben: «Wenn du es in New York schaffst, kannst du es überall schaffen», sang Frank Sinatra in «New York, New York». Für die anderen, die auf der Strecke geblieben sind und in den stinkenden, aber warmen Dunstfetzen der Entlüftungsgitter der U-Bahn leben, ist es der triste Stolz, sich als Ärmste der Armen zu fühlen. «Allein die Tatsache, hier am Leben zu bleiben und jeden Morgen aufzuwachen, gibt mir ein Gefühl des Triumphs», sagte einmal ein «bobo», ein unter seinen Kartons interviewter Clochard. «Jeder Dumme kann als Armer in Kalifornien leben, in New York schaffen das nur die Stärksten».

Für den Touristen kommt dieser Schwindel dem Schauder des städtischen Forschers gleich, eines Stanleys mit Adidas- oder Nike-Schuhen, der nicht auf der Suche nach den Nilquellen unterwegs ist, sondern nach dieser Modernität, die später tropfenweise auch den Rest der Welt erreicht. Da sieht man den Touristen durch Läden schlendern, die davon leben, den Arabern Schmuck zu verkaufen, den Südamerikanern Videogeräte und den Italienern Kleidung, und dabei sucht er die Szenen und Bilder, die er in tausenden von Filmen gesehen hat: die Dunstwolken des «Taxi Driver», die italoamerikanischen Obsthändler des «Padrino», die dunklen «brownstone»-Steinhäuser aus «Manhattan» und die rauchgeschwärzten Ruinen aus «Escape from New York».

Und die Angst, das Wissen um die Brutalität, die an jeder Straßenecke auf der Lauer liegt, verstärkt dieses Schwindelgefühl noch, schärft die Sinne und steigert somit den Genuss. In New York wird alle vier Stunden ein Mensch ermordet, wird alle drei Stunden eine Frau vergewaltigt, wird alle dreißig Minuten ein Raubüberfall begangen und alle 240 Sekunden ein Auto gestohlen. Nichtsdestoweniger suchen die Touristen die Taxifahrer zu überreden, sie nachts nach Harlem zu bringen, sie durchqueren den Central Park zu Fuß und fahren gelassen mit der U-Bahn: mit der sorglosen Verantwortungslosigkeit des Weißen, der sich im Land Rover zur Großwildjagd durch Kenia schaukeln lässt. Nur dass in New York er, der Tourist, die Beute ist.

Der schönste Preis, das kostbarste Souvenir ist, sagen zu können, New York «besiegt» zu haben, stärker und listiger gewesen zu sein als das Stadtmonstrum, das einen verschlingen wollte. Und wenn man in die ruhigen italienischen oder französischen Städte zurückkehrt - wo drei Verbrechen im August gleich zu einem «gewalttätigen Sommer» werden, während in New York 170 Morde im Monat begangen werden -, möchte man ausrufen können, was Jack Lemmon am Ende seines Films «The Out of Towners» ausruft: «Verdammt noch einmal! Du bist nur eine Stadt, und ich bin ein Mensch. Die Menschen sind stärker als die Städte!». Keiner wagt es zu sagen, weder der Bürgermeister noch der Polizeichef, noch die Zeitungen, aber alle wissen es: Die Angst ist einer der großen Magneten, die alljährlich 17 Millionen Besucher anziehen - mehr als das Doppelte der Einwohner New Yorks.

Die letzte, echte Grenze des Exotischen und Wilden ist hier - sicher nicht an den sanften Tropenstränden, die vom Jumbo-Jet-Tourismus vergewaltigt werden, und gewiss auch nicht in den Touristikdörfern eines vom Dollar gezähmten Afrikas. In New York kann man sterben, umgebracht von einem schlaksigen, sympathischen Burschen, dem deine Armbanduhr gefiel oder deine Jacke und der die «saturday night special», den Revolver des Samstagabends, in den Jeans stecken hat. Das hat es gegeben, und das wird es auch in Zukunft geben. In der «Street» von New York, wie sie hier die Börse in der «Wall Street» nennen, kann ein Mann in einem einzigen Jahr - es war 1987 - «Junk bonds» genannte Stücke Papier verkaufen, die nichts anderes waren als Schrott-Obligationen, 425 Millionen Dollar einkassieren und dafür im Gefängnis landen: Sein Name war Mike Millken. In New York kann jeden Augenblick ein Rassen- oder Religionskrieg zwischen Schwarzen und Weißen ausbrechen, zwischen Juden und Nichtjuden, zwischen Koreanern und Puertoricanern, zwischen Moslems und Christen. Bomben sind schon in den Wolkenkratzern des World Trade Center explodiert. Mit Bomben sollten die Tunnel gesprengt werden, die die Insel Manhattan mit dem Festland verbinden. In jeder Sekunde spürt man die Spannung einer Stadt, die ständig am Rand eines tiefen Abgrunds lebt. «Es geht nicht mehr weiter so», sagen die New Yorker. Aber kaum jemand zieht weg. Alle wollen hier bis zum Ende bleiben.

So war es schon immer, seit der Holländer Peter Minuit den Indianern im Jahr 1626 die Insel Manhattan um einen Preis im Wert von 24 heutigen Dollar abkaufte und sie Neu-Amsterdam nannte, als Hauptstadt von Neu-Holland. Die Stadt war schon immer so, hart und brutal, als ihr tyrannischer Gouverneur Peter Stuyvesant sie den siegreichen Engländern abtreten musste, die sie sofort auf New York umtauften, zu Ehren des Herzogs von York, des späteren Königs Jakob II. Sie wurde zu einem Bollwerk der Rebellen gegen die britische Kolonialmacht, als George Washington sie im Jahr 1776 zu seinem Hauptquartier erwählte. Selbst als sie nur fünf Jahre lang, von 1785 bis 1790, als Hauptstadt der neu gegründeten Vereinigten Staaten von Amerika fungierte, wurde sie nicht sanfter. Sie hatte damals nur 30.000 Einwohner, die sich fast alle an der Inselspitze zusammendrängten, wo sich jetzt die Battery befindet, aber sie trug in sich schon den Keim der Stadt, die wir heute kennen.

Als Kaufleute, Versicherungsagenten, Immobilienmakler und Marineoffiziere in Massen ankamen, ersannen die Stadtverwalter im Jahr 1811 den einfachen, von altrömischen Vorbildern übernommenen Grundriss - mit gradlinigen, sich rechtwinklig schneidenden Straßen -, der noch heute die Stärke Manhattans ist. Sie gaben der Stadt diese Gestalt, damit die Fremden und die Neuankömmlinge sich besser orientieren konnten. Während die japanischen Kaiser den Straßen in Kioto und Tokio ihre Namen nahmen, um die Fremden zu verwirren und ihre Gesellschaft noch undurchdringlicher zu machen, öffneten die New Yorker die städtebauliche Struktur, um die Stadt noch leichter zugänglich zu machen. Im Jahr 1830 hatte New York schon 300.000 Einwohner, Ende des 19. Jahrhunderts waren es mehr als anderthalb Millionen. Und die Freiheitsstatue begrüßte mit ihrer gußeisernen Fackel die Massen armer Schlucker, die ankamen, um Tunnel zu graben, Brücken zu schlagen, Wolkenkratzer zu errichten und an Not und Entbehrungen zu sterben. Tausende und abertausende italienischer Auswanderer kehrten zwischen 1880 und 1920 in die Heimat zurück, schockiert von den brutalen Lebensverhältnissen, die sie in New York vorgefunden hatten. «Good riddance», sagten die New Yorker zu ihnen: umso schlimmer für euch. Dieser neue Dschungel nimmt alle auf, aber keiner wird verhätschelt. Wer dieses Schwindelgefühl nicht erträgt, fällt, und nur wenn er Glück hat, verlässt er die Stadt, bevor sie ihn verschlingt. Wer überlebt, bleibt lebenslang ein Opfer. Die Abscheu, die Gewalttätigkeit und die Spannung, die man in New York atmet, gehen einem in Fleisch und Blut über wie die Geometrie der Straßen, die Macht seiner Bauten und das menschliche Bienenstockgewimmel auf der «großen weißen Straße» Broadway oder im «großen schwarzen Dorf» Harlem. Niemand kann den Panoramablick auf Manhattan vergessen, den man vom Empire State Building genießt. Niemand kann das Herzklopfen unterdrücken, das einen überkommt, wenn man erstmals die Skyline der Stadt vom Brooklyn-Ufer aus erblickt: am Abend, wenn die Sonne hinter den Wolkenkratzern von Midtown untergeht, oder wie ich sie von New Yersey aus gesehen habe, in der Nacht der ersten Hundertjahrfeier von Miss Liberty, als Manhattan von den Feuerwerken auf dem Hudson River erleuchtet wurde.

Seit 20 Jahren, seit jenem fernen Augusttag im Jahr 1973, als ich zum ersten Mal auf dem Flughafen Kennedy landete, eine kleine Salamiwurst im Koffer versteckt, um die Zöllner zum Besten zu halten - seit damals suche ich mich von New York zu befreien. Ich habe der Stadt in Büchern und Artikeln alles denkbar Schlechte nachgesagt. Ich verleumde sie, sooft ich kann. Ich hasse sie. Sogar Woody Allen ist mir unsympathisch. Aber ich weiß, dass der Schwindel immer wieder auf mich wartet.

Perhaps it was the sweltering August heat with its pot-pourri of melting asphalt, dampness, vapours and humanity, perhaps it was the weariness imposed by a never-ending journey, the usual delays you learn to expect in summer, compounded by the predictable Customs rigmarole («And what you got stashed away in that bag of yours, Tony? Salami, mortadella, sausages?»). Whatever it was, the first thing I remember about New York and my arrival there twenty years ago can be expressed in a single word: giddiness. The giddiness that comes when you look upwards through rows of valleys seen from below, as though from the floor of a canyon. A giddy whirl of tongues and accents all spoken and shouted together. The giddiness instilled by the hypnotic march of stern vertical and horizontal lines eternally seeking a companion with whom to spawn a right angle, mindless of the curvaceous Baroque and Neo-Classical gentility that makes European cities so easy on the eye. The giddiness of déjà vu, of a city as yet unknown but already seen on countless occasions, as in a recurrent dream that suddenly steps into the real world and grabs you from behind.

Two decades, then, have sped to join the pages of history since I spent my first night in New York, unable to fall asleep nor yet to remain fully awake in a run-down hotel. How many times the bolt and chain on the door of my room must have been ripped off! But that giddiness, that dizziness, that protean vertigo is with me still, and I'm sure it'll be with me for life. I have made my acquaintance with the four hundred and the bovery side of New York. A table at «Le Cirque», Manhattan's most wallet-emptying restaurant, has hosted one with an equal penchant for a mustard-plastered hot dog off some Afghan's or Ethiopian's stall. I've been starry-eyed in the museums, and I've been round the Bronx. I've been mugged and I've listened to Woody Allen playing lousy jazz. I've slept in de luxe hotels and the lofts of friends. Yet I know New York even less than when I arrived for the first time. New York is a metaphor for the whole world. Something there to be experienced, never known.

I've grown fond of my dizziness, like a drunkard with his bottle, a gambler drawn by a roulette wheel. Things people cannot do without, even when they know they'll do them no good. The sensations other cities have to offer are wan and insipid by comparison - the tepid contents of beer bottles opened a week ago. Tokyo is bigger, yet a faceless anthill, as clean as a whistle, with nothing to make your heart skip a beat. Paris is more beautiful, yet remote, with French arrogance oozing from every stone. Rome is soft and melancholic, like a decayed gentlewoman who'll bring out the Spode tea service, and politeness must close your eyes to the chips. London is a monument, the record of a proud past that has faded, leaving naught of service today.

New York, on the other hand, is you and me. Its title deeds bear the name of the world and his wife, its fee simple is shared by all people that on earth do dwell. Africa, for a start, is here in force, two million, one hundred thousand Blacks, mostly concentrated on the other side of the Harlem river at the north end of Manhattan. Little Italy and Chinatown - cities within a city. There are more Jews here than anywhere else on earth. More Ethiopian restaurants than in the whole of poverty-ridden Ethiopia. More Puerto Ricans than in San Juan, the capital of Puerto Rico. And the palette includes a «little Russia», a «little Dublin», a «little Saigon», a «little Warsaw», and a «little Manila».

Woe betide you if you know no French in Paris. Rome and Tokyo lean heavily on Italian and Japanese. In New York, on the other hand, the path from the cradle to the grave needs no English paving stones. Whatever your tongue or dialect, be it Mandarin or Kurd, midwives and doctors, officials and sextons can be found when you are hatched, matched and dispatched. The city yields without demur to the embrace of both the oldest of its citizens and the latest arrival. Millionaire or illegal immigrant, it's all the same. There's no more welcoming place in the world in which to hide or disappear. Those not on easy terms with the law find sanctuary in New York, where crime pays, and how! Only one offence out of ten is punished. Only one robbery every thirty ends up with someone behind bars. And you certainly won't stand out from the crowd because your skin isn't white. People of European descent have now shrunk to a racial minority - only 43% of the 7,322,564 inhabitants of new York's five boroughs: Manhattan, Brooklyn, Bronx, Queens and Staten Island.

Vertigo, therefore, is not a pathological disorder, but the normal, physiological coenaesthesia of those who tread New York's sidewalks. For those who have «made it», for the winners in the rat race towards riches, fame and success, there is the intoxicating thrill of having got the better of the world's harshest city, a degree or an Oscar for survival. As in Frank Sinatra's «New York, New York»: «If you can make it there, you can make it anywhere». And for the losers, those whose portion is the unsavoury, but warmth-giving fumes rising from the gratings of the subway ventilation system, there is a grim pride in feeling a poorer poor bastard and a more trampish tramp than any other down-and-out in the world. «Just to stay alive, here, and wake up again each morning gives me a feeling of triumph», a hobo told me from under his cardboard bedclothes. «Any mug can live on charity in California. Only those who are tough can get away with it in New York».

For the tourist, there is the dizziness of the urban explorer, the latter-day Stanley with Adidas or Nike trainers in search of the sources of another Nile, of that modernity whose trickles and floods wash over the rest of the world. You'll see him on the march, in stores that now only make ends meet by selling jewels to Arabs, video recorders to South Americans, and smartwear to Italians, his eyes scanning the horizon for the scenes and angle shots garnered in a myriad films - the columns of steam in «Taxi Driver», the Italo-American fruit vendors in «The Godfather», the brownstone houses of «Manhattan», or the burnt and blackened ruins of «Escape from New York». Fear, too, and awareness of the brutality in ambush around every corner merely serve to stimulate this giddiness, sharpen the senses and hence the pleasure. A human being is killed every four hours in New York, a woman raped every three, a robbery committed every thirty minutes, and a car stolen every four. Despite all this, tourists try to convince taxi drivers to take them to Harlem at night, cross Central Park on foot, and travel light-heartedly in the subway with the gay foolhardiness of the white man in his Land Rover after big game in Kenya. Here, however, the roles are reversed: the tourist-hunting season is always open.

The prize, the most valuable souvenir, is that of being able to say one has «beaten» New York, that one has been stronger and craftier than this all-devouring urban monster. To be able to cry out at the end of one's trip, when setting off for the quiet cities of Italy and France, where three crimes in August tune all the headlines to the score «summer of violence» (three, for crissake, when there are 170 homicides a month in New York!), like Jack Lemmon at the end of «The Out of Towners»: «Damn you, New York. You're just a city, and I'm a man. Men are stronger than cities». No one dares say so, least of all the mayor, the chief of police and the newspapers, but everyone knows it: fear is the one of the big magnets that attracts 17 million visitors a year to New York, more than two for each one of its inhabitants.

The last, genuine frontier of the exotic, of what is wild and savage, is here, and not for sure on the obedient beaches of tropical localities ravished by Jumbo jet tourism, nor in the tourist villages of a dollar-domesticated Africa. Death lurks in the jungle of New York, maybe at the hands of a gangling, harmless-looking youth who has taken a fancy to your wrist watch or blouson and carries a Saturday night special in his jeans, so that its bullets can provide appropriate payment for these additions to his collection. No traveller's tale this, but one that will have others to keep it company. On Wall Street, or «The Street», as they call it here, a single man raked in 425 million dollars in 1987 through his skilful selling of junk bonds, and was then sent up the river for fraud. His name was Mike Milliken. Race wars can break out from one moment to the next in New York between Whites and Blacks, while religious strife will bring Jews and goyim into conflict, Muslims and Christians, Koreans and Puerto Ricans. Bombs have already exploded in the skyscrapers of the World Trade Center, others had been planned to block the tunnels linking Manhattan to the mainland. Never a second passes without one's sensing the tension of a city permanently perched on the brink of a bottomless abyss. «We can't go on like this», is the general cry. Virtually no one packs up and leaves, however. Everyone wishes to stick it out to the end.

It has always been this way since the Dutchman Peter Minuit bought Manhattan Island from the Indians in 1626 for the equivalent of 24 of today's dollars, and christened it New Amsterdam, capital of New Holland. Harsh andbrutal, too, when its governor, the tyrannous Peter Stuyvesant, had to yield to the victorious British, who promptly replaced Amsterdam with York in honour of the Duke of York, later James II. And it was one of the rebel strongholds against the colonial government when George Washington chose it as his G.H.Q in 1776. Not even a lustrum as capital of the newborn United States from 1785 to 1790 served to confer a gentler sheen. New York had barely 30,000 inhabitants in those days, nearly all packed into the southern tip of the island, where Battery Park is today. The seed of the New York of our times, however, had already taken root.

In 1811, when traders, insurance men, real estate speculators and sea captains began to arrive en masse, the city fathers traced out the simple Hippodamian grid with its Old World pattern of cardines et decumani limites, so dear to the Romans and still the strength of Manhattan. They did so to make it easier for foreigners and new arrivals to move around and get their bearings. At the time when the Japanese emperors were removing the street names in Kyoto and Tokyo to confuse strangers and make their society even more impenetrable, the New Yorkers were opening out the arms of their city and its topography to render it more accesible. By 1830, the thirty thousand had become three hundred thousand, and even this figure was increased more than five-fold by the end of the century. The Statue of Liberty's cast-iron torch lit the way for the masses of desperate beings who came crowding in to dig tunnels, throw out bridges, erect skyscrapers and very often die as the only reward for their toil and privations. Thousands of Italian immigrants returned home between 1880 and 1920, shocked by the brutal living conditions they had found in New York. «Good riddance» were the parting words that echoed in their ears. All are welcome in the new jungle, but there are no red carpets on its floor.

Those who cannot control their dizziness fall. The lucky ones get out before being devoured. Those who survive are victims for life. The horror, violence and tension of New York comes in with every breath and enters your blood, just like the geometry of its streets, the ruggedness of its buildings, the teeming crowd along the Great White Way, or in Harlem, the «great black village». Dull would he be of soul who could forget the view of Manhattan in the round from the top of the Empire State Building, whose heart did not beat a little faster at that first glimpse of the skyline of New York City as seen from the shores of Brooklyn in the evening, when the sun goes down behind the Midtown skyscrapers, or as I saw it from New Jersey on the night of the first centenary of Miss Liberty, when fireworks soared over the Hudson River.

For the last twenty years, since that August day in 1973 when I landed for the first time at Kennedy with a small salami hidden in my suitcase for the sheer hell of it, I have been trying to slough off New York. I have spoken and written harsh words about it in books and articles, and my broadsides are loosed off whenever the occasion arises. I hate it. Even Woody Allen turns me off. However, I know that giddiness awaits me.

Fotos Photographs

David Maria Galardi

1.

2.

1.
Die Freiheitsstatue auf Liberty Island:
im Hintergrund Manhattan.
*The Statue of Liberty on Liberty Island,
with Manhattan in the background.*

2.
Grand Army Plaza zwischen Central Park und der Fifth Avenue.
Grand Army Plaza, between Central Park and Fifth Avenue.

3.
Central Park: Conservatory Pond, Detail der
Bronzegruppe «Alice im Wunderland».
*Conservatory Pond, Central Park. Detail of the
«Alice in Wonderland» group of bronze statues.*

3.

DEER PARK

·NEW YORK·NEW YORK·
·CHRYSLER BUILDING·
·CITICORP BUILDING·
·WATERSIDE PLAZA·

4.
MOMA: das berühmte Museum für moderne Kunst.
MOMA: Museum of Modern Art.

5.
MOMA: das berühmte Museum für moderne Kunst.
MOMA: Museum of Modern Art.

6.
Metropolitan Museum of Art: der Dendur-Tempel.
Metropolitan Museum of Art: Temple of Dendur.

The Waking

◀5./6.

7.
Solomon R. Guggenheim Museum.

8.
Die St.-Patricks-Kathedrale.
St Patrick's Cathedral.

9.
Das AT&T Building an der Madison Avenue.
The AT&T Building, Madison Avenue.

10.
Das Met Life Building (ehemals Pan Am Building).
The Met Life (former Pan Am) Building.

11./14.
Times Square.

15./17.
New York Public Library: Außen- und Innenansicht.
New York Public Library: exterior and interior.

7.

THE SOLOMON R GUGGENHEIM MUSEU

SAINT PATRICK'S
CATHEDRAL

9.

10.

11.

TOMORROW'S
Weather
AIR
COOLER
McDonald's
BILLIONS AND BILLIONS SERVED
OPEN 24 HOURS
EMBASSY 1
ALIVE
McDonald's
sbarro

12.

UNITED ARTISTS
Theatres
Leprechaun
Malcolm X
BODY OF EVIDENCE
DON'T WALK
Roundabout Theatre
110-22
OBJET

13.

Smooth character.
LOW TAR
CAMEL TASTE
GoldStar
AUDIO
VIDEO
COMPUTERS
CAMEL
JOCKEY For Her
...So Comfortable
10 YEARS OF A PERFECT FIT ON A PERFECT "10"
Leone's
Carnevale!
Feb.11-23
UNITED ARTISTS
Theatres
sbarro
the Italian Eatery
CAMERAS - VIDEO
110-220V ELECTRONICS
CANON · NIKON · PANASONIC · OLYMPUS · SONY

14.

ROXY
TWIN
THEATER
4
SMASH
HITS
ONE ADMISSION PRICE
6 NEW XXX MOVIES
EVERY WED SUN
SAFE & COMFORTABLE
NEW CRYSTAL VISION
EVIDENCE

15.

THE LENOX LIBRARY
FOUNDED BY
JAMES LENOX
DEDICATED TO HISTORY
ITERATURE AND THE FINE ARTS
MDCCCLXX

16.

17.

18.
19.▶

MADISON SQUARE GARDEN
ST. JOHN'S BASKETBALL
PRESENTED BY
AMERICAN EXPRESS
/STONY BRK
IMPORTED
NUTS / CANDIES
HOMEMADE
ICE CREAM
Peppermint Park

MADISON

18./19.
Madison Square Garden: sechs Millionen Zuschauer im Jahr.
Madison Square Garden Center: six million spectators a year.

20.
Lincoln Center for the Performing Arts.

21.
Washington Square: im Vordergrund die
«Washington Centennial Memorial Arch».
Washington Square with the
Washington Centennial Memorial Arch in the foreground.

22.
Union Square: Reiterdenkmal für George Washington.
The George Washington equestrian monument in Union Square.

23.
Bauwerke des «Village» (Greenwich Village, SoHo, East Village).
Buildings in Greenwich Village, SoHo and East Village.

21.

22.

23.

24.

25▶

24.
Die Wolkenkratzer von New York: im Vordergrund die «Twin Towers», die Türme des World Trade Center.
New York's skyscrapers with the twin towers of the World Trade Center in the foreground.

25.
Das World Trade Center bei Nacht.
The World Trade Center by night.

26./27.
Battery Park: Fire Dept.

THE BROOKLYN MUSEUM
SCHOOL BUS
9345

28.
Brooklyn Museum.

29.
Queens: die Gleise der U-Bahn.
Das Astoria Building und Manhattan im Hintergrund.
Subway tracks in Queens, with the
Astoria Building and Manhattan in the background.

30.
31.

32.

30./32.
Bronx: der Zoo und der Botanische Garten.
Bronx Park: the Bronx Zoo and the New York Botanical Gardens.

33.
Ditmars Boulevard, Queens.

34.
Yankee Stadium: Number Five: Joe Di Maggio.

35.
Yankee Stadium: Panoramafoto des Inneren.
360° panorama of the Yankee Stadium.

33.
34.►

5
JOE DIMAGGIO
NY
UNIFORM NUMBER RETIRED: 1952
FROM 1936 - 1951,
JOE LED THE YANKEES THROUGH
THEIR MOST DOMINATING ERA.
HIS EXCELLENCE ON THE FIELD
PROPELLED THE BOMBERS TO
TEN WORLD SERIES
AND HIS GRACEFULL STROKE WAS
ONE OF BASEBALL'S GREATEST PLEASURES.

BUD LIGHT

◄35./36.

Nobody beats the
WIZ
FUJIFILM
Getty
PREMIUM
GASOLINES
Rock Solid.
MarketWise.
Prudential Securities
Armitron
HITACHI
ULTRAVISION
BIG BITE
maxell
CHAMP'S

Budweiser

36.
Sarah Lawrence College, Bronxville, Westchester County.

37.

37.
Harlem: das Apollo-Theater, Tempel der schwarzen Musik.
The Apollo Theater, Harlem, temple of black music.

38.
All Saints' Church.

38.

ALL SAINTS
ROMAN CATHOLIC CHURCH
THE THIRD SUNDAY OF ADVENT
REJOICE ALWAYS NEVER CEASE
PRAYING
TODAY IS EDUCATION SUNDAY
WELCOME
BOYS CHOIR OF HARLEM
Phone
Public Pay Telephone

39.

40.

39./40.
Fifth Avenue.

41.
Third Avenue.

42./45.
Die Schaufenster der Madison Avenue.
Shop-windows of Madison Avenue.

46./70.
Menschen in New York.
The people of New York.

ONE WAY

GIORGIO ARMANI
CANALI
CANALI

TO
50%
TICKET
Canon
OLYMPUS
YASHICA
SHARP
ELECTRONICS
CELLULAR TELEPHONES
swatch
SWATCH AUTOMATIC
$65.00
SWATCH SCUBA
49
CANON
49
SWATCH CHRONO
$75

WAITING
LINE
CHASE
Barclay-Rex

CANALI

CHOCOLATE CROISSANT
APPLE TURNOVER
CHERRY TURNOVER
TURKEY CROQUE
CROQUE DU JOUR
BLUEBERRY PIE
SAV-A-RAP

FRANKS
CHICKEN
KEBAB

Grand Central

TAXI FARE
$150 Initial Charge
25¢ Per 1/5 Mile
20¢ Per Minute Stopped or Slow Traffic
50¢ Night Surcharge

MET PHOTO

DIME.

25¢

RUTGERS

65./70.

GIFT OF
UNION OF SOVIET SOCIALIST
REPUBLICS TO THE
UNITED NATIONS
1959
WE SHALL BEAT OUR SWORDS INTO

◄71./72.

71.
Das Gebäude der Vereinten Nationen an der First Avenue.
United Nations Headquarters, First Avenue.

72.
Der Eingang des General Assembly Building.
Entrance to the General Assembly Building.

73./74.
Außen- und Innenansicht des
Gebäudes der Vereinten Nationen.
United Nations Headquarters:
exterior and interior.

73.

74.

75.
76.►

75.
Die Brooklyn-Brücke bei Sonnenuntergang.
Brooklyn Bridge at sunset.

76.
Das Rockefeller Center bei Nacht.
The Rockefeller Center by night.

ROCKEFELLER CENTER

75°

PROMENADE

THE BROOKLYN BRIDGE

MANUFACTURERS HANOVER TRUST
CAMBIO CHANGE WECHSEL

HOTEL EDISON
Canon
SAMSUNG
SAMSUNG
SAMSUNG
SUNTORY
WHISKY
JOHN
RITTER
BORN 1948
Coke
9:40:42
DIGITAL
O & VIDEO
WHAT AMERICA IS SAVING
BY USING MCI INSTEAD OF AT&T
you got the love?
HOWARD JOHNSON'S
ROXY
BURGERS
NOVOTEL
BROADWAY FLEA MARKET
SHUBERT ALLEY

DONT
WALK
FRIDAY'S

Kodak
MARQUIS
MARQUIS THEATRE
MARQUIS THEATRE
MARRIOTT MARQUIS HOTEL
MARQUIS THEATER AND SHOPS

ROCKEFELLER
PLAZA
CROSSING
THE BRIDGE
ONE WAY

Levi's
JEANS FOR WOMEN
VAN WAGNER
FOSTER'S
JVC
QUALITY AUDIO
AND VIDEO
SHOW FOLKS SHOE
"THIS IS WHY BROADWAY W
Newsweek
MARTIN BECK THEATRE 302 W
Panasonic
PALACE
McDonald's
OPEN 24 HOURS
sbarro the Italian Eatery
sbarro
EMBASSY 1
HONEYMOON IN VEGAS
BROADWAY CAMERAS & ELEC
VIDEO CAMERAS
WATCHES
ONE WAY

77.
Der Broadway bei Nacht.
Broadway by night.

78.
Das Empire State Building.
Empire State Building.

79./80.
New York, New York.

78.

79.

80.▶

MetLife
100

81.

82
83

81.
Der Trump Tower an der Fifth Avenue.
Trump Tower, Fifth Avenue.

82.
Das Chrysler Building, 425 Lexington Avenue.
The Chrysler Building, 425 Lexington Avenue.

83.
Das vom Met Life Building reflektierte Chrysler Building.
The Chrysler Building reflected in the Met Life Building.

Seasons Greetings

◄84.
85.

86.

84./86.
Das Rockefeller Center.
The Rockefeller Center.

87.

TIMES SQUARE CHURCH
NONDENOMINATIONAL Revival on Broadway!

88.

OLDEN
FALSETTOS
WEST SIDE THEA

87./90.
Theater am Broadway.
Theaters on Broadway.

89.

90.

金帝国
GOLDEN EMPIRE
珠宝中心
LUCKY JEWELRY CENTER
248
GARMENT DELIVERY

91./92.
Chinatown.

CAFFÈ
DANTE
Reserved
NIGHTLIFE
FINE DINING AWARD
PRESENTED TO

93./95.
Little Italy.

94.

95.

96./97.
Menschen und Wolkenkratzer.
People and skyscrapers.

Famous Name
Men's
Clothing and

◀98./99.

98.
Die Brooklyn-Brücke im Morgengrauen.
Brooklyn Bridge at dawn.

99.
Das Seaport Museum, links Brooklyn.
Seaport Museum, with Brooklyn on the left.

100.
Das Seaport Museum: im Vordergrund der Schoner «Lettie G. Howard», im Hintergrund Manhattan.
Seaport Museum, with the schooner «Lettie G. Howard» in the foreground, and Manhattan in the background.

100.

101.

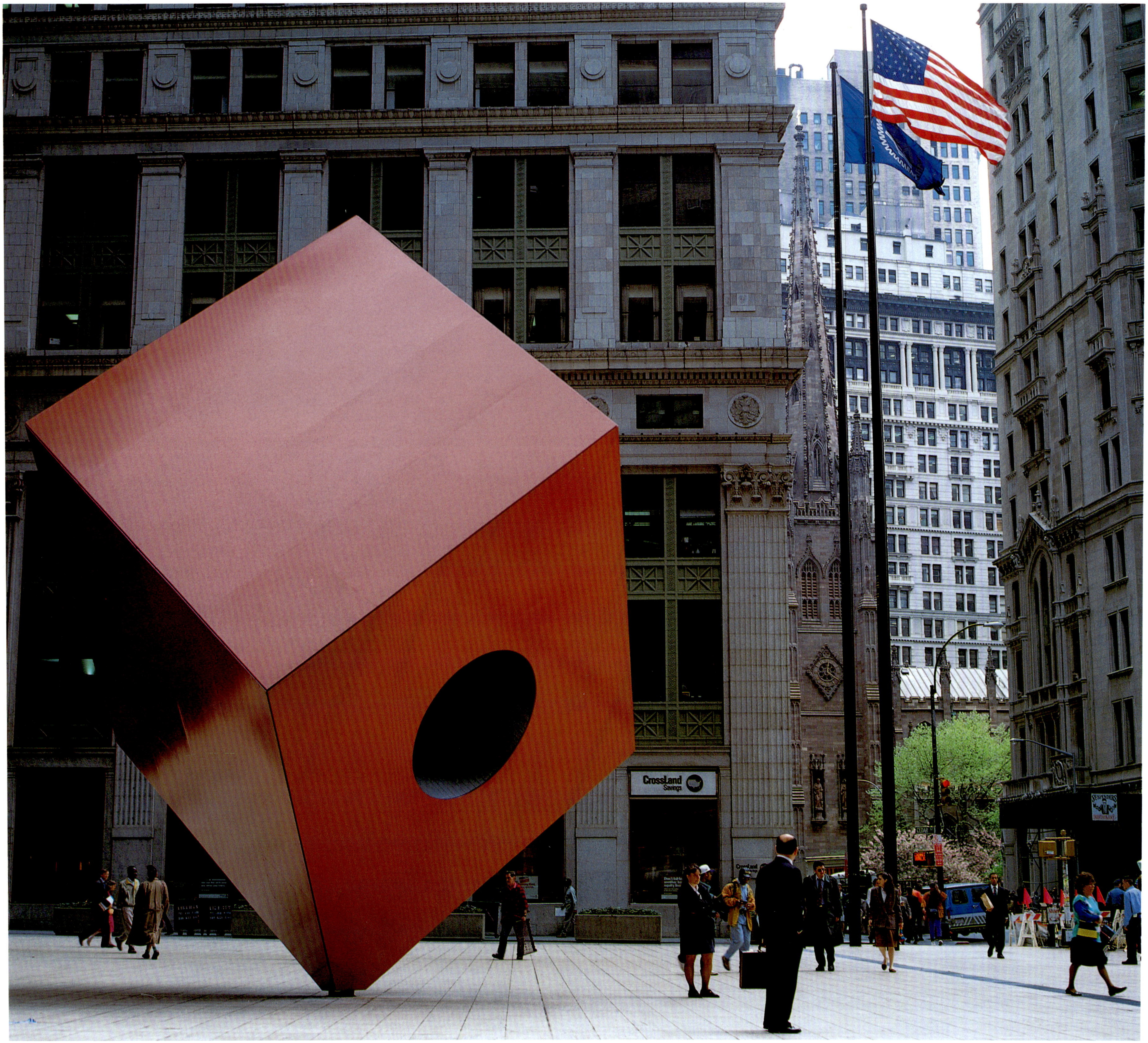

101.
«Cube» von Isamu Noguchi, im Financial District, 140 Broadway.
«Cube» by Isamu Noguchi, 140 Broadway, in the Financial District.

102.
Trompe-l'œil in der Peck Slip.
Trompe-l'œil in Peck Slip.

103./104.
Good-bye, New York.

GRAND ARMY PLAZA
CENTRAL PARK
GET MORE GEAR
1-800-MARLBORO
NYC TAXI
4P48
N.Y.C. TAXI
5Y27
9W52

NO STANDING
M5
LA VIEILLE RUSSIE
ONE WAY
LIBERTOFF

104.

Historische und kunstgeschichtliche Recherchen
Historical and artistic research

David Maria Galardi & Maria Luisa Monti

1.

Knapp unterhalb der Insel Manhattan liegt die kaum weniger berühmte *Bedloe's Island*, auf der die Freiheitsstatue steht, das Symbol für Demokratie und Freiheit. Die Statue, ein anlässlich der Hundertjahrfeier der Vereinigten Staaten geschaffenes Werk des französischen Bildhauers Frédéric-Auguste Bartholdi, war 1886 aufgestellt worden: ein Geschenk der französischen Regierung. In den USA dagegen war das Geld für den Sockel gesammelt worden. Ein Modell dieses Denkmals befindet sich auf einer der Pariser Seinebrücken. Die Statue stellt eine mit einem weich fallenden Gewand bekleidete, stolze junge Frau dar, die in der rechten, nach oben gestreckten Hand eine große Fackel hält, in der Linken dagegen eine Tafel mit dem Datum der Unabhängigkeitserklärung (4. Juli 1776). Sie wiegt 204 Tonnen und ist 46 Meter hoch, während die Fackel sich 93 Meter über dem Sockelfuß befindet. Das aus 300 dünnen Kupferplatten bestehende Denkmal wird von einem von A.G. Eiffel entworfenen Eisengerüst getragen, das auf Stahlsäulen ruht. Mit einem Aufzug können die Besucher durch den Sockel bis zum Fuß des Fundaments fahren, wo sich eine prachtvolle Aussichtsterrasse mit Blick auf den Hafen und Manhattan befindet. Von hier aus kann man auf zwei parallel verlaufenden, spiralförmigen Treppen bis zur Krone hochsteigen. Eine weitere Treppe führt durch den rechten Arm bis zur Fackel, in der sich eine Plattform mit 25 Fenstern befindet. Die Statue, die im Mai 1885 von Frankreich in die Vereinigten Staaten befördert worden war, wurde an der Stelle des früheren *Fort Wood* auf der *Bedloe's Island* aufgestellt, die den schiffbaren Kanal des New Yorker Hafens beherrscht. Sie wurde am 28. Oktober 1886 enthüllt und 1924 vom amerikanischen Kongress zum Nationaldenkmal erklärt. Die Insel wurde 1956 auf den Namen «*Liberty Island*» umgetauft.

Bedloe's Island lies just below Manhattan, yet vies with it in renown, as it is the home of the Statue of Liberty, the world-famous symbol of freedom. Designed by the French sculptor Bartholdi, the statue was presented by France to the United States in 1886. It was paid for by the French people whereras its pedestal was provided by the Americans themselves. A model of the statue was later placed at the end of the Ile des Cygnes on the Seine, in Paris. The subject is a toga'd woman with a great torch in her upraised right hand, and a tablet inscribed with the date 4 July 1776 in the other by her side. She herself is 151 feet high and weighs 200 long tons, whereas the torch is 305 feet from the water level. The statue is composed of 300 thin copper sheets applied to a steel skeleton composed of four columns and designed by Eiffel. A lift rises through the pedestal to the foot of the statue, where a balcony offers visitors a fine view of New York harbour and Manhattan. Two spiral staircases run side by side to the base of the crown on the woman's head, where there is a lookout platform with 25 windows. The statue was brought over from France in May 1885 and erected inside Fort Wood, which once defended the channel leading into the harbour. It was dedicated in October 1886 and declared a national monument by Congress in 1924. The name of the island was changed to Liberty Island in 1956.

◄0 |45° |90° |135° |180° |200° |220° |240° |260° |280° |300° |320° |340° ►360°

2.

Im südlichen Teil des Central Park im Herzen von Manhattan liegt zwischen der Central Park South und der 5th Avenue die *Grand Army Plaza*. Dieser weite, ovale Platz wird von der *Pulitzer Memorial Fountain* und vom exklusiven *Hotel Plaza* beherrscht, das im Jahr 1907 von H.J. Hardenbergh im Stil eines französischen Schlosses errichtet worden war. An der Ecke zur 58th Street befindet sich das Spielwarengeschäft der *F.A.O. Schwarz*, dessen Verkaufserlöse der Unterstützung von Kindern in aller Welt zugewendet werden.

Grand Army Plaza is a large oval area between Central Park South and Fifth Avenue in the southern part of Central Park in the heart of Manhattan. It is the home of the Pulitzer Memorial Fountain and the Hotel Plaza, built in the style of a French castle in 1907 by H. J. Hardenbergh and one of the most exclusive in the world. Schwarz, the FAO's toyshop on the corner of 58th Street, directs the proceeds of its sales to helping throughout the world.

3.

Der 340 Hektar große *Central Park* dehnt sich zwischen der *59th Street* und der *110th Street* im Herzen von Manhattan aus. Seine Lage und seine Größe machen ihn zu einer der bekanntesten und meistbesuchten Grünanlagen unter den mehr als hundert New Yorker Parks. In den Sommermonaten sind der Zoo, der Shakespeare-Garten, die *Mall*, die Gewächshäuser, das Stadion für Freilichtkonzerte und die vielen Sport- und Spielplätze des Central Park beliebte Ziele der in Scharen herbeiströmenden Besucher. Im Park stehen viele Denkmäler und Statuen, und hier befinden sich auch mehrere Seen und Teiche: Besonders zu erwähnen sind darunter der *Pond*, ein Schutzareal für Wasservögel, und der *Conservatory Pond*, an dessen Ufer sich die Statue des dänischen Schriftstellers Hans Christian Andersen und die Bronzegruppe «Alice im Wunderland» befinden.

Central Park extends from 59th to 110th Street in the center of Manhattan Island and covers an area of 840 acres. It is the best known and the most frequented of New York's more than 100 parks. In the hot summer months, crowds of visitors come to see the zoo, the Shakespeare Garden, the Mall, the greenhouses, the open-air concert stadium and the many playing-fields and sports grounds. The Park has a goodly crop of statues and monuments. There are also a number of lakes. The Pond is the preserve of water fowl. The Hans Andersen statues and the Alice in Wonderland bronze group stand beside the Conservatory Pond.

4.

Das berühmte *Museum of Modern Art MOMA* war 1929 mit der Absicht gegründet worden, hier einzig Werke moderner Kunst aus der Zeit nach 1880 zu sammeln. In den ersten Jahren konnten nur wenige Werke ausgestellt werden, bei denen es sich überwiegend um Leihgaben handelte. Dank der Schenkungen der zwei weiblichen Gründungsmitglieder Bliss und Rockefeller und der späteren Umgestaltung und Erweiterung des Gebäudes mit den Einnahmen der Licht- und Luftrechte eines 58stöckigen Wolkenkratzers, der über dem Museum erbaut worden war, konnte die Ausstellungsfläche auf die heutigen vier Stockwerke ausgedehnt werden. Zum musealen Bestand gehören außer reichen Skulpturen- und Gemäldesammlungen auch eine umfangreiche Fotogalerie und zwei Abteilungen für Zeichnungen und Illustrationen. Ein ganzes Stockwerk steht im Zeichen des modernen Designs auf den Gebieten Architektur, Einrichtung, Automobil und Gebrauchsgegenstände und zeigt deren Entwicklung vom Ende des 19. Jahrhunderts bis heute.

The Museum of Modern Art (MOMA) was inaugurated in 1929 to house works of art from 1880 onwards. It began with only a few items, mostly on loan. Later donations from Ms. Bliss and Ms. Rockefeller, two of its founder members, coupled with the restructuring and extension rendered possible by the income received from an easement of air and light granted when a 58-storey skyscraper was built alongside it, enabled it to double its exhibition space, which now occupies four floors. The Museum's extensive painting and sculpture collections have been joined by a photography section, two autographed drawings sections, and a whole floor devoted to the development of design since the end of the 19th century in the fields of architecture, furniture, motor vehicles and everyday objects.

5.

Beim *Metropolitan Museum of Art* handelt es sich um das größte Museum Amerikas und das drittgrößte der ganzen Welt (nach dem British Museum in London und der Eremitage in Petersburg). Es wurde 1870 von einer Künstlergruppe gegründet und befindet sich seit 1880 an der jetzigen Stelle. Der an der *5th Avenue* gelegene Hauptbau wurde zu Beginn des 20. Jahrhunderts eingeweiht. Zum Bestand des Museums, das durch Stiftungen ständig bereichert wird, gehören mehr als drei Millionen Kunstwerke, und obwohl es über 300 Ausstellungsgalerien besitzt, kann immer nur ein Viertel der Schätze gezeigt werden. Das mächtige Bauwerk umfasst Sammlungen von unschätzbarem Wert: Malereien, Skulpturen, Möbel, Stoffe, Rüstungen und andere Kunstwerke aus allen Zeiten und allen Ländern der Welt. Bemerkenswert sind die Sammlungen griechischer, ägyptischer und römischer Antiken, die einen vorzüglichen Einblick in diese Kulturen vermitteln.

This is America's largest museum and the third largest in the world after the British Museum and the Hermitage in St Petersburg. Founded by private initiative in 1870, it was eventually located in Central Park. The main building on 5th Avenue was inaugurated at the turn of the century. The collections are composed of over 3,000,000 items. Not more than a quarter can be displayed at any one time, even though there are more than 300 galleries. Priceless paintings, sculptures, prints, furniture, fabrics, armour and objets d'art from every period of history and from every part of the world are on display. Egyptian, Greek and Roman art are well represented.

6.

Während der Bauarbeiten des Assuandamms in Ägypten musste der aus dem 1. vorchristlichen Jahrhundert stammende Tempel der Dendur vor der Überflutung durch den Stausee gerettet werden. So beschloss die ägyptische Regierung, ihn den Vereinigten Staaten zu schenken, wo er im *Metropolitan Museum of Art* rekonstruiert wurde. Der Tempel, ein Teil der reichen ägyptischen Sammlung, befindet sich in einem eigens errichteten Glashaus.

The 1st century B.C. Temple of Dendur was presented to the United States by Egypt to save it from being submerged for ever when the Asswan Dam was built. It has been put together piece by piece in the Metropolitan Museum of Modern Art and located in a building of its own with glass walls and a glass roof.

7.

Das *Solomon R. Guggenheim Museum* ist das einzige von Frank Lloyd Wright entworfene Museum und der einzige von ihm für New York konzipierte Bau. Das «Schneckenhaus», ein vorzügliches Beispiel funktioneller Architektur, besteht aus einer spiralförmig verlaufenden Rampe mit 3% Gefälle, die den Besucher zu den 70 Nischen und Schauräumen führt, in denen sich die Kunstwerke befinden. Das originell gestaltete Innere, das durch Tages- wie durch Kunstlicht erhellt wird, bietet ideale Ausstellungsverhältnisse. Den Grundbestand des Museums bilden die Privatsammlungen des Industriellen und Kunstmäzens S.R. Guggenheim mit Arbeiten von Künstlern des 19. und des 20. Jahrhunderts. Diese Werke sind heute nur noch gelegentlich und in einem kleinen Teil des Museums zu sehen, da fast die gesamte Ausstellungsfläche von den jährlich fünf oder sechs großen Sonderschauen eingenommen wird.

The Solomon F. Guggenheim Museum is the only museum designed by Frank Lloyd Wright, and also the only one of his works in New York. This example of functional architecture has a spiral ramp with a 3% slope. The visitor walks along a route that takes him down past 70 niches and small galleries. The interior is lit by both natural and artificial light, and its original form enables the works of art to be viewed in a systematic and panoramic manner. The Museum's permanent collection is primarily composed of the Salomon R. Guggenheim bequest, i.e. the private collection built up by its founder, which consists of works by 19th and 20th-century artists. Nowadays however, these are exhibited only occasionally and in a small part of the Museum, because nearly all the space available is devoted each year to five or six special exhibitions.

8.

Die bekannteste der katholischen Kirchen in New York ist die an der *5th Avenue* gelegene *St.-Patricks-Kathedrale.* Der neugotische Bau aus der zweiten Hälfte des 19. Jahrhunderts, heute Sitz der römisch-katholischen Erzdiözese von New York, war 1910 dem irischen Nationalheiligen Patrick geweiht worden. Die über 100 m hohen Zwillingstürme, die acht Meter große Rosette und das reich verzierte Eingangsportal bilden besonders bei Nacht einen faszinierenden Kontrast zu den ringsum aufragenden Wolkenkratzern. Das Gewölbe des stimmungsvollen Innenraums, der 2500 Sitzplätze aufweist, ruht auf hohen Marmorsäulen, und das Licht fällt durch große Fenster in das Hauptschiff, in das Querschiff und auf den Hauptaltar. Die Kunstwerke der Kathedrale wurden überwiegend von europäischen Künstlern geschaffen.

St Patrick's Cathedral on Fifth Avenue is New York's best known Roman Catholic place of worship and the seat of its archibishop. Built in the Neo-Gothic style in the second half of the 19th century, it was dedicated to the patron saint of Ireland in 1910. It has two slender bell towers 330 ft high on either side of the façade, a rose window 26 ft in diameter, and a storiated portal. These features naturally form a striking contrast with the skyscrapers all around, especially at night. The interior can seat 2500 persons. Its vaults rest on stout marble piers, while large stainedglass windows throw a flood of light into the nave and transept, and onto the high altar. Most of the ornaments are European in style.

9.

Am südlichen *Broadway* liegt auf der Höhe der *55th Street* und der *56th Street* der Hauptsitz der *American Telephone and Telegraph Company*, ein 195 m hohes Gebäude aus gelb-rosa Granit, das zum Symbol der Wolkenkratzerarchitektur der Achtzigerjahre geworden ist. Typische, wenn auch umstrittene Merkmale sind der ungewöhnliche Giebel und das sechs Stockwerke hohe Eingangsportal. Die in der Eingangshalle aufgestellte Statue des *Golden Boy* ist das Sinnbild der modernsten Fernmeldetechnik. Im *TA&T Building* befinden sich außer den Verwaltungsbüros auch ein Auditorium, wo 32 synchronisierte Videoprojektoren dreidimensionale Illusionseffekte schaffen, und das *Infoquest Center*, das über die jüngsten Technologien aus dem Informatikbereich informiert.

The American Telephone and Telegraph Building stands between 55th and 56th Street in the most crowded section of the southern part of Broadway. A symbol of skyscraper architecture in the Eighties, it is in yellow-pink granite and rises to a height of 645 ft. Completed in 1983, its post-modern style is underscored by the striking front with its soaring entrance arch – 110 ft high, the equivalent of six storeys – and has been the subject of lively discussion. The Golden Boy statue (the «Spirit of Communications») is set in the centre of the foyer. In addition to the Company's offices, the building also has an auditorium, where 32 synchronised video projectors are used to create imaginary 3-D effects, and the Infoquest Center, where the latest information technologies are on display.

10.

Das 58stöckige, 246 m hohe *Met Life Building*, das sich an der Kreuzung *48th Street/Park Avenue* erhebt, war 1963 als Sitz der Fluggesellschaft Pan Am errichtet worden. Das Gebäude, das heute als klassisches Beispiel der amerikanischen Wolkenkratzerarchitektur der zweiten Generation gilt, war während der Bauarbeiten heftig kritisiert worden, da es den Blick auf einen Teil der *Park Avenue* versperrte. In der weiten, öffentlich zugänglichen Eingangshalle sind Werke vieler zeitgenössischer Künstler zu sehen. In den Achtzigerjahren wurde der Bau von einer Versicherungsgesellschaft erworben.

This 58-floor, 810-ft high building was completed in 1963 as the home of Pan American World Airways, and sold to the Met Life insurance company in 1989. It is located at the junction of Park Avenue and East 42nd Street. This example of a second-generation skyscraper was harshly criticised during its design and erection on the grounds that its bulk would block the view along the whole of Park Avenue. Works by many contemporary artists are on display in the large entrance hall, which is open to the public.

11.

12.

13.

14.

Der Platz am Schnittpunkt von *Broadway*, *7th Avenue*, *West 42nd Street* und *West 47th Street* war bis ins frühe 20. Jahrhundert als *Longacre Square* bekannt: ein Platz mit Ställen, Pferden und Kutschen, der Treffpunkt von Droschkenkutschern und Hufschmieden war. Im Jahr 1904 ließ der Verleger der «New York Times» an der Südseite dieses Platzes das neue Verlagshaus errichten, damals das zweithöchste Gebäude der Stadt, und den Platz in *Times Square* umbenennen. Schon 1883 war hier der erste Sitz des *Metropolitan Opera House* eingeweiht worden, zwei Jahre später entstand das *Olympic Theater*, und als in dieser Gegend kurz nacheinander viele neue Theater eröffnet wurden, ging der Stadtteil als *Theater District* in die New Yorker Geschichte ein. Weiteren Ruhm brachten dem *Times Square* die hier erbauten Hotels ein, die von Schauspielern, Schriftstellern und Kunstkritikern besucht wurden. In jüngster Zeit bemüht sich die Stadtverwaltung um ein Comeback des Platzes, der in den vergangenen Jahrzehnten etwas in Vergessenheit geraten war, aber seinen ursprünglichen Charme beibehalten soll.

At the beginning of the 20th century, the long section where Broadway crosses Seventh Avenue between West 42nd Street and West 47th Street (then known as Longacre Square) was flanked by livery stables and farrieries, while cab ranks and waiting carriages, harness makers and other evidence of the twilight of the era of the horse abounded. In 1904, the New York Times erected a tower building to house its new publishing headquarters on the south side of the square. At the time, this was New York's second highest edifice, and the square began to acquire the name of the newspaper. The first home of the Metropolitan Opera House had been inaugurated on the same side in 1883, and the Olympic Theater was erected there two years later. The area around, in fact, soon became known as the Theater District as a string of other playhouses took the hint, while several leading hotels frequented by actors, men of letters and art critics added to the lustre and renown of Times Square. Its recent past, however, has been a far cry from these former splendours. Efforts are now being made to plan a better future for the Square without detracting from its original charm.

15.

16.

17.

Die *New York Public Library*, nach der *Library of Congress* in Washington die zweitgrößte Bibliothek der Vereinigten Staaten, ist - ihrem Namen zum Trotz - eine Privateinrichtung, die nur zur Hälfte von öffentlichen Geldern finanziert wird. Die New York Public Library, die aus der Fusion von drei privaten Bibliotheken (der *Astor Library*, der *Lenox Library* und der *Tilden Foundation*) hervorgegangen ist, befindet sich in einem Ende des 19. Jahrhunderts aus Vermont-Marmor errichteten Bau. Sie besitzt ungeheuer viele Bücher und Dokumente, zu einem großen Teil Nachschlagewerke, die man mit Hilfe von computerisierten Karten einsehen kann, während man für Originalmanuskripte und Buchraritäten eine Sondergenehmigung braucht. Besondere Kostbarkeiten der *Public Library* sind eine Gutenbergsche Bibel und eine autographische Kopie von Thomas Jeffersons Unabhängigkeitserklärung. Hochinteressant sind auch die Kinderbuchabteilungen und die Sammlungen fremdsprachiger Literatur.

The New York Public Library, which despite its name is only 50% supported out of public funds, is the second largest in the States after the Library of Congress in Washington. It came into being as a result of consolidation of the privately owned Lenox and Astor Libraries together with the Tilden Foundation trust, and is housed in a building made of Vermont marble erected at the end of the 19th century. The library's immense stock of volumes (mostly encyclopædias) can be consulted in the reading rooms in a few minutes by means of computerised cards, whereas permission is needed to examine rare books and MSS. The *pièces de resistance* include a copy of the Gutenberg Bible, and a copy of the Declaration of Independence bearing the signature of Thomas Jefferson. There are also sections devoted to children's literature, and large collections of works in foreign languages.

18.

19.

Beim *Madison Square Garden* handelt es sich um eine der größten Veranstaltungsstätten, die jemals in einer Stadt errichtet worden sind. Die Arena ist die geeignete Bühne für sportliche Veranstaltungen, Rodeos und Zirkusvorstellungen, für Reitturniere und Eishockeyspiele, aber auch für politische Versammlungen und Rockkonzerte. Der Rundbau kann in wenigen Stunden aus einem Eislaufpalast in einen mit 600 Tonnen Erde bedeckten Spielplatz verwandelt werden.

Madison Square Garden is one of the largest arenas constructed within a city. It is the home of sports events, rodeos, circuses, equitation competitions, ice-skating shows, political rallies and rock concerts. The floor can be changed in a few hours from a skating rink into a playing field covered with 600 tons of earth.

20.

Zwischen der 61th und der 66th Street liegt am *Broadway* das *Lincoln Center for the Performing Arts*, das in sechs Bauten die bedeutendsten New Yorker Kultureinrichtungen beherbergt: das *New York Philharmonic Orchestra*, die *Metropolitan Opera Company*, die *Lincoln Repertory Company*, das *New York State Theater*, die *Juilliard School of Music* und die *Library and Museum of the Performing Arts*. Als erster Teil des *Lincoln Center*, das auf dem riesigen Areal eines Ende der Fünfzigerjahre abgerissenen Slums angelegt worden war, konnte 1962 die *Philharmonic Hall* eröffnet werden, die - wie auch die in den darauf folgenden Jahren eingeweihten Kulturstätten - mit italienischem Travertin verkleidet ist. In der Mitte des Kulturzentrums tut sich, der *Columbus Avenue* gegenüber, die *Lincoln Center Plaza* auf, die im Sommer zum Schauplatz von Straßentheater-Performances wird.

The Lincoln Center's six main buildings are the homes of the New York Philharmonic Orchestra, the Metropolitan Opera Company, the Lincoln Repertory Company, the New York State Theater, the Juilliard School of Music, and the Library and Museum of the Performing Arts. A large slum area was cleared to make for the centre at the end of the Fifties, and the Avery Fisher Hall (for the Philharmonic) was the first building to be opened in 1962. Like the others, which were soon completed, it is faced with Italian travertine. The «Plaza», an open space between the three largest buildings and facing Columbus Avenue, is the stage for «street theatre» performances in the summer.

21.

Der *Washington Square* ist der Hauptplatz im Herzen des *Greenwich Village*. Dieser Ort, in vergangenen Jahrhunderten eine Oase der Ruhe, ist heute für die Einheimischen wie für die Einwanderer aller Rassen und Länder eine ideale Stätte zum Musizieren, Spielen, Sonnen und Rollschuhlaufen. Den Platz beherrscht der *Centennial Memorial Arch*, ein Triumphbogen, der 1892 anlässlich des 100. Jubiläums der Wahl von George Washington zum ersten USA-Präsidenten (1789) errichtet worden ist. Am *Memorial Arch* beginnt die sieben Meile lange *5th Avenue*, die durch die New Yorker Stadtmitte verläuft. Der Platz, auf dem 1888 ein Denkmal für Garibaldi aufgestellt worden ist, wird von den Bauten der *New York University* gesäumt.

Washington Square is now partly incorporated within Greenwich Village. As in the 19th century, it is a pleasure ground for people of every kind, who come to sunbathe, roller skate or put on impromptu musical shows. The Centennial Memorial Arch half-way along the north side of the Square is the starting point of Fifth Avenue, which runs for seven miles through the heart of New York. This triumphal arch was erected to commemorate the first centenary of the election of George Washington as the first president of the United States (1789), and was finished in 1892. The Square is surrounded by buildings forming part of New York University and also serves as its campus. A statue of Garibaldi was erected near the centre of the Square in 1888.

22.

Der mit seinen Parkanlagen im Jahr 1830 eröffnete *Union Square* war zu Beginn des 20. Jahrhunderts, als ihn große Hotels, viele Theater und elegante Geschäfte umgaben, das New Yorker Vergnügungsviertel, zugleich aber auch ein bekannter Treffpunkt der Radikalen. Im Laufe der Zeit verlor er seine Anziehungskraft. Heute aber sind die jahrzehntelang verwahrlosten Grünanlagen wiederhergestellt worden, und mit neuen Geschäften, Hotels, Büros und Wohntürmen sieht der Platz einer besseren Zukunft entgegen.

Originally laid out as a park in 1830 on what was then the edge of New York, Union Square was later bordered by shops and places of entertainment. In the early decades of this century, it was often the scene of public meetings and demonstrations. New shops, hotels, offices and residential tower blocks now surround the gardens, which have been revived after many years of neglect.

23.

Das *Greenwich Village* ist für die New Yorker schlechthin «The Village». Im frühen 17. Jahrhundert hatten sich hier Indianer niedergelassen, die dann von den Holländern vertrieben wurden. Auf sie wieder folgten die Engländer, die das Dorf in ein elegantes Wohnviertel verwandelten. Der Stadtteil wurde zu Beginn des 20. Jahrhunderts als Treffpunkt der New Yorker Bohemiens bekannt. Berühmte Maler, Sänger, Musiker und Dichter ließen sich in die-

The area comprising «The Village» as it is usually called, was occupied by the Indians at the beginning of the 17th century when the Dutch began to arrive, while at its end a small village had formed, named after one near London, since New York was by now a British colony. The Village's bohemian history began just before the first world war, when low rents attracted an influx of painters, singers, musicians and poets, and lasted well into the Thirties in the hands

ser stadtfernen Oase nieder. An einigen Häusern sind auch Gedenktafeln zu finden, die an ihre illustren Bewohner erinnern. Heute ist das *Greenwich Village* ein Wohnviertel, wo neben modernen Bauten immer noch kleine, alte Steinhäuser anzutreffen sind.
Als das *Greenwich Village* zu einem Intellektuellentreff wurde, siedelte die weniger wohlhabende Bevölkerung in weiter östlich gelegene Gebiete um. Um den *St Mark's Place* entstand das *East Village*, das zur Heimat der «Blumenkinder» wurde. Im späten 19. Jahrhundert hatten in dieser Gegend vorwiegend Deutsche und Ukrainer gelebt. Viele von ihnen mussten - oft gegen ihren Willen - ihre Häuser an Bauunternehmer abtreten, die hier Nobelbauten und Luxusläden entstehen ließen, sodass Reichtum und Armut in diesem Stadtviertel bis heute nebeneinander fortleben.
SoHo (SOuth of HOuston Street), das im Süden an das *Greenwich Village* anschließt, ist aus einem alten Lagerhausviertel hervorgegangen. Heute ist es das Reich der Kunstgalerien und der Jazz- und Rocklokale, der exklusiven Boutiquen und der extravaganten *Open-Space*-Häuser der Künstleravantgarde. Einzig in SoHo sind die typischen «Cast Iron Houses» zu finden, die vor über hundert Jahren errichteten Gusseisenbauten, die als früheste Beispiele von Fertigbauten angesehen werden können und heute - wie das ganze Stadtviertel - unter Denkmalschutz stehen.

of the «lost generation». Plaques recalling those days can be seen on some of the few small masonry houses that still survive among the modern residential edifices and shops. East Village, where many intellectuals now prefer to live, is the name that has been given for the last thirty years or more to an area beside Second Avenue crossed by St Mark's Place Street and others with a host of boutiques and foreign restaurants. It was the original home of the «flower children» movement. The local population was mainly composed of Germans and Ukrainians at the end of the 19th century, most of whom sold out, often against their will, to builders of luxury apartments and shops. Both poverty and ostentation of wealth, indeed, are still very evident. SoHo (SOuth of HOuston Street is an area beside Little Italy and separated from Greenwich by the West Houston Street that has contributed to its name. Until some forty years ago, it was mostly composed of warehouses and small factories, many of which were subsequently taken over by avantgarde artists, seeking plenty of well-lit, open space for their studios. Today, there are many art galleries, boutiques and jazz and rock halls. SoHo's main claim to distinction, however, is its preservation of many examples of cast-iron architecture, the original form of prefabricated construction used on a wide scale, especially at the end of the 19th century, prior to the advent of the skyscraper era. The whole area is thus the subject of very close environmental protection.

24.

Als die Grundstückspreise gegen Ende des 19. Jahrhunderts immer mehr anstiegen, mussten die amerikanischen Architekten notgedrungen «in die Höhe gehen». Die ersten Wolkenkratzer wurden ganz aus Stein erbaut und hatten entsprechend dicke Wände. Dann aber setzten sich dank der technologischen Entwicklung im frühen 20. Jahrhundert zuerst der Stahl und dann der Stahlbeton durch. Sie ermöglichten die Anlage mehrstöckiger und zudem leichterer und schlankerer Bauten, die zur stilistischen Autonomie der amerikanischen Architektur beigetragen haben. In den Dreißigerjahren gewann eine funktionelle Bauweise an Boden, dank der die Raumplanung in den Großstädten grundlegend erneuert werden konnte. New York und besonders Manhattan sind beredte Beispiele dafür. Anfangs wurden ausschließlich turmförmige Wolkenkratzer errichtet (*Chrysler Building, Empire State Building*, usw.). Doch als in die schluchtartigen Tiefen zwischen den Bauten kaum noch Luft und Licht eindringen konnten, ging man zur Planung von treppenförmigen Gebäuden über, die sich gegen oben hin verjüngen. Angesichts des Baubooms der letzten Jahrzehnte sah sich die New Yorker Stadtverwaltung allerdings gezwungen, eine größere Distanz zwischen den einzelnen Wolkenkratzern vorzuschreiben - was zu einer sonderbaren Gewohnheit geführt hat: Die Besitzer von niedrigeren Gebäuden verkaufen den Bauunternehmern die Lichtrechte über ihrem Besitztum. Sie leben zwar im Schatten, können aber hohe Gewinne verbuchen. Das *MOMA* (Foto 4) hat auf diese Weise seine Erweiterungsbauten finanzieren können.

Around 1890, land became so expensive in New York that architects were forced to build upwards. The first skyscrapers were made of stone with very thick walls. The 20th century, however, soon offered steel and then reinforced concrete as much more pratical alternatives, resulting in the construction of slimmer and even higher buildings. By the Thirties, American architecture had reached a functional style all its own that changed the planning of urban space within a metropolis. New York, and Manhattan in particular, show how this style developed. Initially, the preference was for skyscrapers in the form of towers, such as the Chrysler and Empire State Building, but as the spaces between them grew ever narrower to become chasms shut off from sufficient light and air, there was a switch to edifices of gradually diminishing volume. The building boom in recent years, however, has made it necessary for the authorities to prescribe a greater distance between one skyscraper and another. This has given rise to a practice whereby the owners of lower buildings sell the rights to the space over their properties, and thus get handsomely paid for living in the shade. As mentioned earlier (photo 4), the Museum of Modern Art resorted to this arrangement to finance the substantial extension of its premises.

◄0 |45° |90° |135° |180° |200° |220° |240° |260° |280° |300° |320° |340° ►360°

25.

Die *Twin Towers*, die 110stöckigen, 410 m hohen Zwillingstürme, gehörten zum 1977 eingeweihten *World Trade Center*, das auch das *Southeast Plaza Building* und das *U.S. Customs Building* mit dem *Zollmuseum* und dem *Information Service* umfasste. Sie lagen um die *Austin J. Tonbin Plaza*, auf der ein großer Brunnen mit der Skulptur «Der Globus» von Fritz König steht. Die *Twin Towers*, die mit ihren Fundamenten zwanzig Meter tief in das Schiefergestein eindrangen, hatten einen quadratischen Grundriss mit 63 m Seitenlänge und Aluminiumfassaden mit mehr als 43.500 Fenstern. Von der Aussichtsplattform des südlichen Zwillingsturms konnte man einen atemberaubenden Rundblick auf die ganze Stadt genießen; ähnlich faszinierend war die Aussicht aus dem Restaurant «Windows on the World», das sich im 107. Stock des Nordturms befand.

The twin 110-storey, 1345-foot tall towers of the World Trade Center inaugurated in 1977 form part of a complex that includes two plaza buildings and the U.S. Customs House with its museum and information service, as well as a hotel, set around the Austin J. Tonbin Plaza, which has a large bronze globe by the German sculptor Fritz Konig revolving in the centre of a fountain set in the midst of trees. The foundations of the towers go down over 65 feet into the slate bedrock to support buildings with a 206x206 ft ground plan and aluminium curtain walls pierced by over 43,500 windows. The observation deck of Two World Trade Center, as the south tower is called, offers a superb view of the city. This is located on the 107th floor, like the «Windows on the World Restaurant» in One World Trade Center, which provides another breath-taking panorama.

26.

27.

An der Südspitze von Manhattan liegt direkt am *Hudson River* der grüne *Battery Park*. In seiner Nähe erwächst derzeit das hochmoderne Wohn- und Geschäftsviertel *Battery Park City*, das an Größe einzig dem *Rockefeller Center* nachsteht. Auf der dem *Hudson River* zugewandten Seite zieht sich eine breite, zwei Kilometer lange Promenade hin. Das *Fire Department Museum* am Südende der Insel dokumentiert die Geschichte der Feuerwehr. Ein neben dem Museum aus dem Wasser auftauchendes Denkmal erinnert an die Rettung Schiffbrüchiger.

Battery Park with its avenues and trees is set beside the Hudson River at the southernmost tip of Manhattan. A short distance away, a huge new residential, shopping and business quarter called Battery Park City is being established. Second in size to the Rockefeller Center, it is flanked on the river side by an esplanade over a mile long. The Fire Department Museum on the southern tip recounts the history of the Fire Brigade, while a monument beside it commemorates the rescuescues carried out at sea.

28.

Das *Brooklyn Museum* kann zwar mit nicht so hohen Besucherzahlen aufwarten wie die Museen in Manhattan, gehört aber mit seinen Kunstsammlungen aus dem Orient, dem Vorderen Orient und Ägypten zu den Highlights auf diesem Gebiet. Das Erdgeschoss bietet Ausstellungen primitiver indianischer, afrikanischer und präkolumbianischer Kunst, im ersten Stock werden Kunstwerke aus dem Orient und dem Vorderen Orient gezeigt, während im zweiten Stock, wo sich auch die *Wilbour Library of Egyptology* befindet, Originalwerke der koptischen, ägyptischen, griechischen und römischen Kultur zu sehen sind. Besonders interessant sind im dritten Stock die 25 im Stil des 17. bis 19. Jahrhunderts eingerichteten Räume und ein rekonstruiertes Haus aus der holländischen Kolonialzeit in Brooklyn mit zeitgenössischen Geräten und Gegenständen. Der «Skulpturengarten» im Museumshof birgt Bauteile, die in erster Linie von abgerissenen Häusern in Manhattan stammen. Neben dem *Brooklyn Museum* befindet sich das *Children's Museum*, das 1899 als erstes Museum dieser Art gegründet worden ist.

The Brooklyn Museum does not receive as many visitors as those in Manhattan. Even so, its Oriental, Middle East and Egyptian art sections are strong. The ground floor is devoted to primitive art from Africa and Pre-Columbian North and South America. The first floor covers the Middle and Far East. Assyrian, Egyptian and Coptic, Greek and Roman antiquities are displayed on the second floor, which is also the home of the Wilbour Library of Egyptology. The 25 rooms on the third floor are furnished and decorated in styles ranging from the beginning of the 17th to the middle of the 19th century. The reconstruction of a house in Brooklyn itself inhabited by a Dutchman in the 17th century with its period furnishings and utensils is of particular interest. The museum's Sculpture Garden contains an impressive collection of lintels, capitals and other architectural bits and pieces salvaged from buildings demolished in Manhattan. The Children's Museum lies about a mile to the east. It was founded in 1899 and is the first of its kind in the world.

29.

33.

Zu *Queens*, dem größten der fünf Stadtteile von New York City, gehören die Wohnviertel *Flushing*, *Forest Hill* und *Kew Gardens*, und hier liegen auch der La-Guardia-Flughafen und der internationale Flughafen John F. Kennedy. Das derzeitige *Queens* war ursprünglich um 1635 von Holländern besiedelt worden. Im Jahr 1683 wurde es der englischen Provinz New York angeschlossen und zu Ehren der Königin Katherina von Braganza, der Gemahlin Karls II. von England, auf den Namen getauft, den es bis heute trägt. Im Jahr 1898 kam es zu New York.

Queens is the largest of New York's five boroughs. It is primarily a residential area composed of several well-known districts, such as Flushing, Forest Hills and Kew Gardens, though it is also the home of both the La Guardia National and the John F. Kennedy International airports. The Dutch began to settle here around 1635. When New York became a British colony, the name Queens was conferred on the area in honour of Catherine of Braganza, wife of Charles II of England. It became part of New York City in 1898.

30.

31.

32.

Von den fünf New Yorker «boroughs» ist der Stadtteil Bronx der einzige, der ganz auf dem Festland liegt. Sein Name geht auf den dänischen Einwanderer Jonas Bronck zurück, der sich hier 1639 als erster niedergelassen hatte. Der Stadt New York wurde er im Jahr 1898 angeschlossen. Der *Bronx Park* ist eine der ausgedehntesten und ältesten Grünanlagen New Yorks. In der Bronx, durch die der gleichnamige Fluss fließt, sind bis heute noch gut erhaltene, historisch interessante Bauten anzutreffen. Beim *Hemlock Forest* handelt es sich um den Überrest eines riesigen Waldes, der zur Zeit der Algonkin-Indianer die ganze Halbinsel bedeckte. Der *Bronx Park* umfasst im Süden den *Botanical Garden*, einen der ältesten botanischen Gärten der Vereinigten Staaten. Auf einer 117 Hektar großen Fläche beherbergt er außer reichen Pflanzen und Blumen aus aller Welt auch das *Enid-A.-Hampt*-Gewächshaus mit Tropenpflanzen und Wüstenlandschaften, das *Herbarium*, ein Museum, eine Bibliothek und ein Forschungslabor. Ebenfalls zum *Bronx Park* gehört der *Zoo*, wo Vögel, Affen, Reptilien, Pinguine und Gorilla in modernen Freigehegen leben, die ihrem natürlichen Lebensraum so gut wie möglich nachempfunden sind.

The Bronx is the only one of New York's five boroughs that does not form part of an island. It takes its name from a Danish immigrant who was the first to settle here in 1639, and is a hilly, mostly residential area that also became part of New York City in 1898. Bronx Park is one of the largest and oldest in New York. It is crossed by the Bronx river and contains some old buildings in a good state of repair. The Hemlock Forest is all that remains of the thick woods that covered the peninsula at the time of the Algonquin Indians. The northern half of the Park consists of the New York Botanical Garden. One of the oldest in the United States, its more than 40 acres are planted with trees and flowers from many parts of the world, especially in the Herbarium and the huge Enid A. Hampt Conservatory with its tropical species and desert settings. There is also a museum with a library and research laboratory in the grounds. The Bronx Zoo occupies the southern half of the Park. It is composed of both open enclosures and houses for birds, monkeys, reptiles, penguins and gorillas, and their natural habitats have been established as far as possible.

34.

◄ 0 |45° |90° |135° |180° |200° |220° |240° |260° |280° |300°

35.

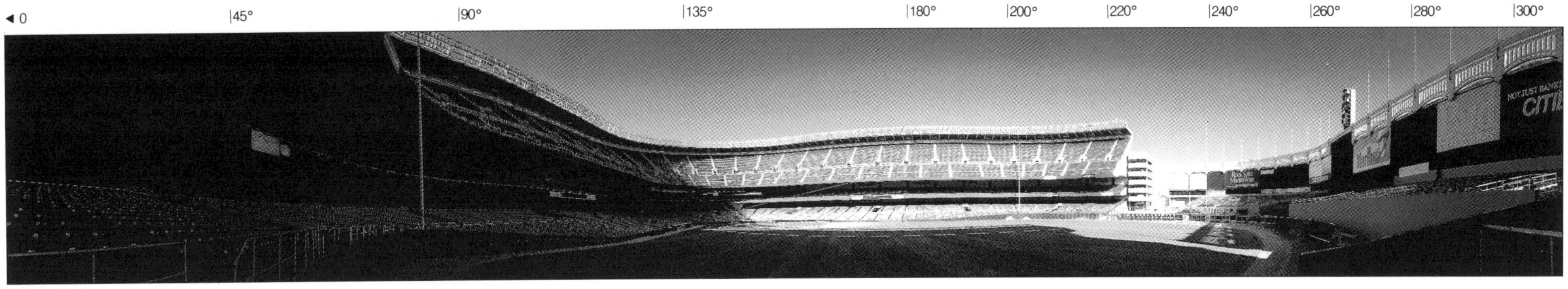

Der Baseball ist der in den USA verbreitetste Sport, ja, er kann geradezu als Nationalsport angesehen werden. Schon achtjährige Kinder beginnen auf Straßen und Höfen Baseball zu spielen, treten dann bald - als Amateure oder als Profis - in Sportvereine ein, und Baseballplätze gibt es in allen Stadtparks. Die zwei berühmtesten New Yorker Mannschaften sind die «Yankees», die in der 1900 gegründeten American League spielen, und die «Mets», die der 1876 entstandenen National League angehören. Das *Yankee Stadium* war bei seiner Eröffnung im Jahr 1923 das größte Baseballspielfeld der Vereinigten Staaten, und zu Ehren des Starschlägers Babe Ruth wurde es als «House that Ruth Built» bezeichnet. Im Yankee Stadium wird auch die Erinnerung an Joe Di Maggio lebendig erhalten, der von 1936 bis 1952 bei den Yankees spielte (diese Mannschaft konnte 1941 einen Rekord verzeichnen, als sie hintereinander 56 Matchs gewann). Sein Name befindet sich seit 1955 neben den berühmtesten Baseballspielern aller Zeiten in der *«Baseball Hall of Fame»* in Coppertown.

As everyone knows, baseball has long been America's national sport. Children begin by knocking a ball around in the yard when they are about eight years old, and can then work their way up through a series of professional or amateur leagues. There is a ballfield in Central Park and many other smaller parks. New York's two leading teams are the Yankees, who play in the American League (created in 1900), and the Mets, who play in the National League (founded at Boston in 1876). The Yankees Stadium was built in 1923. The largest of its day in the States, it was affectionately dubbed the «House that Ruth built» in honour of the great batter Babe Ruth. Joe Di Maggio, who played for the Yankees from 1936 to 1952, is also commemorated in the stadium, and his name was added to baseball's Hall of Fame at Coopertown in 1955. In 1941, the Yankees won 56 games in a row, one of the major records in the League's history.

36.

In *Bronxville*, einem Städtchen 15 Meilen nördlich von New York City, befindet sich das *Sarah Lawrence College*, eine 1926 gegründete, freie Kunstuniversität. Sie verfügt über eine Bibliothek mit 288.000 Büchern, ein *Performing-arts*-Center, mehrere Theater, Konzertsäle und Kinos, Kunstgalerien, Musikbuchhandlungen und Aufnahmestudios, und sie wird von 700 Studentinnen und 250 Studenten besucht, die in eigenen Zimmern im *Campus* wohnen. Dem Lehrkörper gehören mehr als 200 Dozenten an (sodass auf jeweils 3-4 Studenten ein Lehrer kommt), die zweiwöchige Vorlesungen und Seminare abhalten, wobei die Studenten ihren Studiengang nach eigenem Belieben zusammenstellen können. Der Kunstgeschichtsunterricht findet direkt im *Museum of Modern Art* statt, und dank lebhafter Kontakte zu den namhaftesten Universitäten der Welt können die Studenten auch Studienjahre in Oxford, London, Moskau, Paris und Florenz belegen und an Sommerkursen an den Universitäten Michigan, London und Florenz teilnehmen.

Bronxville, a small town 15 miles north of New York City, is the home of the Sarah Lawrence College, a free university for the arts founded in 1926. It has a library with 288,000 books, a performing arts centre, theatres, concert halls, cinemas, art galleries, music libraries and recording studios. About 700 women and 250 men live on the campus as full-time students. The teaching staff is composed of more than 200 members. Seminars and lectures are held twice a week, and the students plan their own curricula. Art courses are conducted in the Museum of Modern Art, while arrangements with foreign universities enable undergraduates to spend an academic year at Oxford, London, Moscow, Paris and Florence. Summer courses are given at the University of Michigan, as well as in London and Florence.

37.

38.

Der Stadtteil *Harlem* dehnt sich nördlich der *110th Street* aus, und er wird im Westen vom Hudson River und im Osten vom Harlem River eingeschlossen. Er wurde 1658 von Holländern unter der Führung von Peter Stuyvesant erstmals besiedelt und behielt seinen ländlich-dörflichen Charakter bei, bis er sich zu einem Wohnviertel der Mittel-Oberklasse entwickelte, als die Bahnverbindung mit der Südspitze der Insel Manhattan hergestellt wurde. Vom frühen 20. Jahrhundert an wurden die Wohnungen zunehmend an Afroamerikaner vermietet, die aus den Slums im Süden hierher gezogen waren, und schon 1910 galt Harlem als «schwarzes» Wohnviertel. In halb verfallenen Häusern leben hier bis heute noch viele Arbeitslose. Neben in jüngster Zeit errichteten Gebäuden sind hier auch noch bestens erhaltene und gut restaurierte Wohnbauten zu finden, die auf die Zeit um 1891 zurückgehen, besonders an zwei der schönsten Straßen von New York: an der *138th* und an der *139th*, die heute als *Strivers' Row* bekannt ist. Sehenswert sind die vielen Kirchen, darunter die *Abyssinian Baptist Church* und die *All Saints' Church*, die vom Architekten der St.-Patricks-Kathedrale entworfen worden ist. Das 1913 eröffnete *Apollo Theater* wurde bald zum Jazztempel, durfte aber bis in die Dreißigerjahre nicht von Schwarzen betreten werden. Später sind hier die berühmtesten schwarzen Musiker aufgetreten, wie Duke Ellington, Count Basie, Dizzy Gillespie und Aretha Franklin.

The district known as Harlem lies between the Hudson river on the west and the Harlem river to the east, and stretches northwards from 110th Street. The Dutch governor Peter Stuyvesant founded the village of Niew Haarlem in 1658 and the area remained rural until the arrival of the railway from the lower half of Manhattan transformed it into an elegant residential quarter with brownstone houses inhabited by upper middle class families. In later years, a shift of the Black population from the South in search of better wages resulted in increasing occupation of the tenementsments of Harlem, and it was not long before no white inhabitants were left. Harlem today has many semi-derelict buildings occupied by large numbers of mostly unemployed persons. All this gives the zone the appearance of a ghetto, though in effect it is less delapidated than others. Indeed, there are modern edifices recently erected alongside restored buildings dating back to 1891, especially those on two of New York's most attractive streets, 138th and 139th (now called Striver's Row). There are numerous churches, including the Abyssinian Baptist and All Saints', designed by the architect who designed St Patrick's Cathedral. The Apollo Theater – the temple of jazz – was inaugurated in 1913. Until the Thirties, coloured persons were not admitted, but later famous black musicians performed there, such as Duke Ellington, Count Basie, Dizzy Gillespie and Aretha Franklin.

39.

40.

41.

42.

43.

44.

45.

Die *Fifth Avenue*, und besonders der zwei Kilometer lange Teil zwischen der *34th* und der *59th*, gilt als eleganteste Straße von New York. Hier reihen sich Luxusboutiquen, Bankhäuser von Weltrang und die Verwaltungsbüros der meisten internationalen Fluggesellschaften aneinander, und zu den berühmtesten Bauten gehören das *Rockefeller Center*, die *Public Library*, das *Empire State Building* und Kirchen wie die *St.-Patricks-Kathedrale*. Die *Fifth Avenue*, die Manhattan in einen westlichen und einen östlichen Sektor teilt, stellt einen großen Anziehungspunkt für Touristen wie für Einheimische dar. Die vielen Volksgruppen, die in der Stadt leben, halten auf dieser Straße gern Paraden ab, weshalb sie oft für den Verkehr gesperrt ist. Parallel zur *Fifth Avenue* verlaufen die *Madison Avenue* und die *3rd Avenue*. Mit ihren Haute-Couture-Ateliers und den berühmtesten Schmuck- und Antiquitätenläden der Welt, die auch am Wochenende und oft bis spät in die Nacht hinein offen bleiben, sind sie heute die begehrteste Shoppingmeile der Stadt. In der *West 47th* ist zwischen der *Fifth Avenue* und der *Avenue of the Americas* der Diamantenhandel zu Hause, während sich die *West 46th* zu einem Klein-Brasilien entwickelt hat. Von der Ecke *Fifth Avenue/43rd Street* genießt man einen besonders eindrucksvollen Blick auf das *Chrysler Building*.

Fifth Avenue's fame as New York's most elegant street and the location of luxury shops, banks, airline offices and renowned buildings, such as Rockefeller Center, the Public Library, the Empire State Building and St Patrick's Cathedral stems from the mile and a half section between 34th Street and 59th Street. The full length of the Avenue, in fact, divides Manhattan into a western and an eastern sector. In the absence of large squares, too, it forms intersections with the roads that cross the island, while its width and popularity make it a favourite for parades by ethnic groups, and it is often closed to traffic. Madison Avenue and 3rd Avenue run parallel to Fifth Avenue on its east side, and are also lined with boutiques, jeweller's and antique dealer's shops that stay open during the weekend, as well as in the late evening by turns. The block that stretches along West 47th Street from Fifth Avenue to Sixth Avenue (Avenue of the Americas) is known as Diamond Row. West 46th Street has become a sort of little Brazil. A particularly fine view of the Chrysler Building can be obtained from the intersection between Fifth Avenue and 43rd Street.

Bei einem Bummel durch New Yorks Straßen kommt man mit einem wahren, sich ständig wandelnden Mosaik aus Farben, Formen und Licht in Berührung. Auf den Straßen sind Leute unterwegs, die allen Rassen angehören, sich auf unterschiedlichste Art und Weise kleiden, Sprachen und Dialekte aus allen Ländern der Welt sprechen. Man sagt, dass in New York mehr Juden leben als in Israel, dass die Nachkommen der Italiener inzwischen die Einwohnerzahl einer Stadt wie Rom erreicht haben, dass es hier genauso viele Iren gibt wie in Dublin und mehr Deutsche als in Bremen. Aber groß ist auch die Anzahl der Afroamerikaner, und die Zahl der Südamerikaner hat sich in den vergangenen zehn Jahren verdreifacht. Bei Tag verschmelzen alle diese Personen, die sich auf Straßen und Plätzen drängen, in Parks und Büros, in der U-Bahn und in den Kirchen, zu einem bunten, anderswo unvorstellbaren Kaleidoskop.

The streets of New York offer a continually changing kaleoidoscope of colours, shapes and lights, since they are peopled by men and women whose origins, tongues and apparel can be traced to many other parts of the world. It is said that there are more Jews in New York than in Israel, as many «Italians» and «Irish» as there are in Rome and Dublin, and more «Germans» than in Bremen. There are also many Africans and the number of South Americans has trebled over the last ten years. It is a very heterogeneous mixture, therefore, that forms the daytime population of New York's thoroughfares, plazas, parks, offices, churches and subway trains.

46.

47.

48.

49.

50.

51.

52.

53.

54.

55.

56.

57.

58.

59.

60.

61.

62.

63.

64.

65.

66.

67.

68.

69.

70.

71.

72.

73.

74.

Der Gebäudekomplex der *Vereinten Nationen* liegt im östlichen Manhattan zwischen der *First Avenue* und dem *East River*. Er wird vom 154 m hohen, *Secretariat Building* beherrscht, einem 39stöckigen, schlanken Wolkenkratzer, der eine Fassade aus Aluminium und grünblauem Glas und Seitenwände aus kräftigem Vermont-Marmor besitzt und die New Yorker Skyline mitprägt. Zur Anlage des 1952 eingeweihten Gebäudekomplexes hatten außer der Stadt New York auch Privatpersonen sowie amerikanische und ausländische Organisationen beigetragen. 1946 hatte John D. Rockefeller den ersten Geldbetrag zum Kauf eines Grundstücks bereitgestellt, die New Yorker Stadtverwaltung schenkte das angrenzende Areal, Dagmar Hammarskjöld, der zweite UNO-Generalsekretär, unterstützte die Gründung der Bibliothek, und die amerikanischen Kinder stifteten den Brunnen. Das Gebiet, auf dem sich die UNO-Bauten erheben, genießt Exterritorialität, weshalb es hier eine eigene Polizei und ein Sonderpostamt gibt.
Die UNO-Vollversammlungen finden im *General Assembly Building* statt, einem Marmor-Kalkstein-Bau mit sieben von Kanada geschenkten Nickel-Silber-Portalen, die in eine weite Eingangshalle mit einer von Griechenland gestifteten Zeusstatue führen. Ein an der Decke hängendes Pendel macht die Bewegung der Erde deutlich. Eine Freitreppe steigt zum ellipsenförmigen Sitzungssaal der Generalversammlung an, der fast so breit ist wie ein Fußballfeld. An der Decke, unter der ein siebenstöckiges Haus Platz hätte, tut sich eine einen Meter weite Öffnung auf, durch die ein einziger Sonnenstrahl in das Kuppelinnere fällt. Seitlich der Eingangshalle befindet sich ein kleiner *«Meditation Room»*, der Delegierten und Besuchern aller Religionen zugänglich ist. Die offiziell verwendeten Sprachen sind Chinesisch, Arabisch, Englisch, Französisch, Russisch und Spanisch. Die Vereinten Nationen haben es sich zum Ziel gesetzt, für den Frieden in der Welt und die internationale Sicherheit zu wirken. Zu diesem Zweck greifen sie als Mittler zwischen verfeindeten Staaten ein. Ihre wichtigsten Organe sind die Generalversammlung, der Sicherheitsrat, der Wirtschafts- und Sozialrat, der Treuhand-Verwaltungsrat, der Internationale Gerichtshof und das Generalsekretariat. Besondere Abteilungen beschäftigen sich mit Problemen von internationaler Tragweite wie der Ernährung, der Landwirtschaft, der Gesundheit und der Arbeit.

The group of buildings forming the Permanent Headquarters of the United Nations Organisation lies between First Avenue and the East River. The main edifice is the Secretariat Building, a slim, 39-storey skyscraper about 500 feet high whose two façades are in aluminium clad with tinted blue-green glass, while the two side walls are made of Vermont marble. Contributions from the U.S. Government, the City of New York, American and foreign associations and private sources went into the construction of the Headquarters, most of which was finished by 1952, whereas the Hammarskjold Library was added in 1961 in memory of the U.N.'s second secretary-general. A large sum was given for the purchase of land by John D. Rockefeller Jr. in 1946, and other land alongside was donated by the City of New York. The marble fountain in front of the Secretariat Building was donated by the children of America. The area occupied by the Headquarters enjoys extraterritorial rights and has its own police force and post office. The General Assembly Building is a delightfully tapered edifice made of marble and limestone. Its sloping roof is crowned by a cupola. Seven nickel-silver entrance doors presented by Canada give access to the Main Lobby, where there is a statue of Zeus donated by Greece. A pendulum suspended from the ceiling indicates the rotation of the Earth. The oval Assembly Hall is reached via a staircase. It is about half as wide as a football pitch. A lantern four feet in diameter in the seven-storey high ceiling allows a single ray of sunlight to enter the cupola. There is a small meditation room beside the Main Lobby for the use of visitors and delegates of every faith and persuasion. The official languages of the United Nations are English, French, Spanish, Russian, Arabic and Chinese. The aim of the United Nations system is to work for peace and international security by bringing its member states together. Its main task is to mediate between nations in conflict. Its principal organs are the General Assembly, the Security Council, the Economic and Social Council, the Trusteeship Council, the International Court of Justice, and the Secretariat. Other specialised agencies are concerned with matters of international importance, such as food, agriculture, health and labour.

◄ 0 |45° |90° |135° |180° |200°

75.

Die 1052 m lange *Brooklyn Bridge*, die älteste Brücke über den *East River*, verbindet Manhattan mit Brooklyn. Sie wird von zwei mächtigen Granitpfeilern getragen und verläuft 40 Meter über dem Fluss. Besonders am frühen Morgen und bei Sonnenuntergang bietet diese Hängebrücke stimmungsvolle Ausblicke auf New York und seine Wolkenkratzer, auf den Hafen *South Street Seaport* und die *Upper Bay* mit der *Freiheitsstatue* im Hintergrund.

The Brooklyn Bridge is the oldest bridge over the East River. It runs from the New York Civic Center (which includes City Hall) to Brooklyn Heights. Its single 3450-foot span is suspended by cables from granite pylons and rises about 135 feet above the water. At sunset and in the early morning, the Bridge offers fine views of Manhattan, the old South Street Seaport and Upper New York Bay with the Statue of Liberty in the background.

◄0 |45° |90° |135° |180° |200° |220° |240° |260° |280° |300° |320° |340° ►360°

76.

84.

85.

86.

Zwischen der *Fifth Avenue* und der *Avenue of the Americas* ist in den letzten 60 Jahren das *Rockefeller Center* entstanden, eine Wolkenkratzerstadt in der Stadt, die das Bild von Manhattan verändert hat. Initiator war John D. Rockefeller jr., der damals reichste US-Bürger, dem viele Wohlfahrtseinrichtungen in den USA zu verdanken sind. Das ursprünglich aus 14 Bauten bestehende *Rockefeller Center* wurde 1954 erweitert, sodass es heute auf mehr als 20 Gebäude kommt, mit Büros, Restaurants, Geschäften, Fernsehstudios und unterirdischen Ausstellungsräumen. Das Bauensemble schmücken außen wie innen Skulpturen, Fresken und Basreliefs. An der *Rockefeller Plaza* ragt das 250 m hohe *R.C.A. Building* auf, hinter dem die *Radio City Music Hall* liegt, der größte Theatersaal der Welt. Von der *Rockefeller Plaza*, auf der häufig farbige Fahnen wehen, gelangt man zur tiefer gelegenen *Sunken Plaza* mit einer Prometheusstatue aus vergoldeter Bronze. Besonders im Sommer wird dieser Platz zum belebten Treffpunkt der Menschen, die in den umliegenden Geschäften und Büros arbeiten. Im Winter verwandelt er sich in eine Eislaufbahn, und zu Weihnachten wird hier ein mindestens 20 m hoher, reich geschmückter Tannenbaum aufgestellt.

The Rockefeller Center is a conglomeration of skyscrapers and other buildings lying between Fifth Avenue and Seventh Avenue in the heart of Manhattan. It began life some sixty years ago, but started to acquire its modern appearance in 1954. Offices, restaurants, shops and radio and TV studios occupy most of the space, and there are many exhibition galleries in the Concourse, a labyrinth of downstairs malls. Sculptures, frescoes and bas-reliefs adorn both the exterior and the interior of the Center. The RCA Building (850 feet) is the tallest of the Center's towers and is entered from Rockefeller Plaza. The world's largest auditorium is in the Radio City Music Hall Entertainment Center. Behind it on the other side of West 50th Street, Rockefeller Plaza is often decked with flags. Lower Plaza beside it is a sunken esplanade with a gilded bronze statue of Prometheus on one side. It is very crowded, especially during the summer, because it is the natural rendez-vous for the Center's office workers and shop assistants. During the winter, an ice rink is installed and a gaily decorated Christmas tree some 70 feet high is set up every year.

◂ 0 |45° |90° |135° |180° |200°

77.

87.

88.

89.

90.

Eine Schlüsselstraße zum Verständnis von New York City ist der weltberühmte, 30 km lange *Broadway*, der sich als einziger Boulevard durch ganz Manhattan zieht. Er beginnt am *Battery Park*, führt durch das weite Handels- und Finanzdistrikt um die *Wall Street* und kreuzt auf der Höhe der *42d Street* den *Times Square*. In dieser Gegend schlägt das Herz der New Yorker Showindustrie, mit unzähligen Theatern, Kinos und Nightclubs, und die vielen Reklameschilder haben dem hier fast taghell erleuchteten Broadway den Beinamen *«Great White Way»* eingebracht. Weiter im Norden führt der *Broadway* an der *Columbia University* vorbei, um dann den *Harlem River* zu überqueren und als Autobahn *U.S. 9* am Ostufer des *Hudson River* zu verlaufen. Aber beim Namen Broadway denkt man vor allem an das Theaterdistrikt: Die teuersten *On-Broadway*-Theater liegen direkt am Broadway, die weniger teuren bis billigen Spielstätten, die als *Off-Broadway*- und *Off-Off-Broadway*-Theater bezeichnet werden, befinden sich in den umliegenden Areals zwischen der *41st* und der *62nd Street*, und alle zusammen tragen sie zur führende Rolle New Yorks in der amerikanischen Theaterszene bei.

The name Broadway conjures up the notion of theatres and cinemas. The road itself, however, is 18 miles long. It begins at the north end of Battery Park and runs the whole length of Manhattan along a course that brings it over to West Side, and takes it on beside Columbia University and the Hudson River until it crosses the Harlem river to pass right through the Bronx and become State Highway No. 9. Its first short stretch runs through the business district and past Wall Street. Its central section between West 42th Street and 53rd Street is often called «The Great White Way» because it is so brilliantly lit at night. Broadway and Times Square are like Siamese twins from West 42nd to West 47th Street (see Nos. 12-15), and surrounded by «On Broadway» theatres, cinemas and night clubs. The terms «Off Broadway» and «Off-Off Broadway», indeed, are used for smaller, less expensive theatres well outside this «Theater District», mainly in SoHo, Greenwich and East Village, and the Upper East and West Sides.

78.

Im Jahr 1931 wurde nach nur 14monatiger Bauzeit das 102stöckige *Empire State Building* fertig gestellt, der damals höchste Wolkenkratzer der Welt. Er ist 381 m hoch (mit der Antenne sogar 449 m), 72 Aufzüge verbinden im Inneren die Etagen, und von den zwei Aussichtsplateaus - dem Aussichtsdeck im 86. Stock und dem Freiluftplateau im 102. Stock - genießt man unvergleichliche Ausblicke nicht nur auf Manhattan, sondern auch auf die anderen New Yorker Stadtteile und bis nach New Jersey hinüber. Bei starkem Wind hört man das Stahlgerüst des leicht schwankenden Gebäudes knarren. Die Fenster des Kalkstein-Granit-Baus bestehen aus rostfreiem Stahl, die oberen 30 Stockwerke sind jede Nacht beleuchtet, und dank der vier mächtigen, «Freedom Lights» genannten Scheinwerfer an der Spitze ist das Gebäude aus 130 km Entfernung, von Flugzeugen sogar aus 480 km Distanz zu erkennen.

Erected in less than two years and inaugurated in May 1931, the 102-storey Empire State Building was the tallest skyscraper in the world for many years. The edifice itself is 1250 feet high and is served by 72 lifts, whereas the total height is taken to 1450 feet by a TV aerial. There is an open observation platform on the 86th floor, and an enclosed terrace on the 102nd floor, both of which obviously provide a superb panorama of the whole of New York itself and New Jersey on the other side of the Hudson. On windy days, one can hear the steel beams creak as the building sways slightly. The body of the edifice is composed of limestone and granite, while its stainless-steel window-frames shine by day and at night, when four beacons called the «Freedom Lights» can be seen 80 miles away from the ground, and as much as 300 miles by aircraft.

79.

80.

Die Hektik und der Trubel der Großstadt scheinen unendlich fern, wenn man New York von der Spitze eines Wolkenkratzers betrachtet. Man glaubt zwischen Traum und Wirklichkeit zu leben, zwischen Vergangenheit und Zukunft, fühlt sich in eine verzauberte Welt ohne Gegenwart versetzt. Der Rhythmus des Alltags wird langsamer, und alle Hast weicht einer ruhigen Gelassenheit.

The hustle and bustle of the great metropolis seems far away, half-dream, half-reality, when viewed from the top of a skyscraper. One's thoughts turn to the past or the future, and the present is forgotten. The pace of life is slowed down, creating a state of suspended animation that soothes the mind.

81.

Der im Jahr 1983 vollendete, 58stöckige und 202 m hohe *Trump Tower* an der *Fifth Avenue* ist zweifellos der spektakulärste der in jüngster Zeit errichteten Wolkenkratzer. Der Fußboden und die Wände der wunderschönen Eingangshalle bestehen aus rosafarbenem italienischem Marmor, und vom 13. Stockwerk stürzt ein künstlicher Wasserfall herab. Im Erdgeschoss befinden sich einige Restaurants und exklusive Geschäfte, in den oberen Stockwerken Büros und Apartments, bis hinauf zur noblen Dachwohnung, die für etliche Millionen Dollar vermietet wird.

Completed in 1983, Trump Tower, on Fifth Avenue, is certainly the most spectacular member of the latest generation of skyscrapers. It is 663 feet high and its 58 floors are occupied by busy shops and restaurants, offices and then apartments rented at enormous sums, especially in the uppermost storeys. The foyer of the Tower is among the finest of many in New York. It is six storeys high and its walls and floor are in pink Italian marble. There is also a 78-foot waterfall.

82.

83.

Das *Chrysler Building* erhebt sich an der Ecke *Lexington Avenue/Fifth Avenue*, nicht weit vom Bahnhof *Grand Central Terminal* entfernt. Es wurde 1930 vollendet und war mit seinen 319 Metern ein Jahr lang, bis zur Fertigstellung des *Empire State Buildings*, das höchste Bauwerk in New York. Bis heute ist es das höchste unter Denkmalschutz stehende Gebäude der Vereinigten Staaten geblieben, und als ein Musterbeispiel der Art déco ist es von weit her an seinen Stahlbogen und den dreieckigen Fenstern zu erkennen. Auch wenn sich New York inzwischen mit höheren und moderneren Wolkenkratzern präsentieren kann - das *Chrysler Building* steht bis heute einzig dar und ist einer der romantischen Symbolbauten New Yorks geblieben.

Erected in 1930 on the corner of Lexington Avenue and East 42nd Street and a stone's throw from Grand Central Terminal, the Chrysler Building's 1046 feet made it the city's tallest building for just a year until the Empire State was finished. It is still the highest national monument in the States. Its prestige stems from its fine *art déco* hall, its steel arches and its triangular windows, which make it easily recognisable from any part of the city. Taller, more modern skyscrapers, such as the two World Trade Center towers, now lord it over New York. The Chrysler, however, is the only one of its kind and has lost none of its glamour.

91.

92.

Die ersten chinesischen Einwanderer hatten sich 1847 in New York niedergelassen, aber ein massenhafter Zustrom an Chinesen setzte mit der im Jahr 1965 erfolgten Änderung der bis dahin rigorosen Einwanderungsgesetze ein, und auf dem relativ begrenzten Areal von *Chinatown* siedelten sich tausende von Orientalen an. *Chinatown*, heute die größte chinesische Stadt außerhalb Chinas, breitet sich immer mehr im südlichen Teil Manhattans aus. Die Bewohner dieser exotischen Stadt in der Stadt sind in hunderten von Restaurants, Lebensmittelgeschäften und Wäschereien tätig. In *Chinatown* gibt es buddhistische Tempel, ein chinesisches Museum und Kinos, in denen Filme aus Hong Kong und Taiwan in Originalsprache vorgeführt werden, und hier erscheinen auch mehrere Tageszeitungen in chinesischer Sprache, die unterschiedliche politische Tendenzen widerspiegeln. Faszinierend ist das chinesische Neujahr, das mit lebhaften Paraden, Drachen, maskierten Tänzern und prächtigem Feuerwerk gefeiert wird.

Chinese settlers first came to New York in 1847. The main influx, however, began when the immigration laws were made less stringent in 1965. Chinatown itself is small, but is the home and workplace for thousands of Chinese. Its population, indeed, makes it the largest Chinese town outside China itself. An exotic character is conferred on this slowly expanding quarter by its many restaurants, food shops and laundries, Buddhist temples, a Chinese museum, and cinemas showing films from Hong Kong and Taiwan in Chinese. There are also several Chinese dailies with different political leanings. The best time to visit Chinatown is on the Chinese New Year's Day (first full moon after 19 January), when the streets are filled with colourful processions, dragons and lions, and masked dancers, accompanied by showers of fireworks to drive off evil spirits.

93.

94.

95.

Nordwestlich von Chinatown liegt *Little Italy*, einer der kleinsten ethnisch geprägten Stadtteile New Yorks. Heute leben hier noch die Italoamerikaner der älteren Generation - die Jüngeren zieht es mehr an den Stadtrand -, und nachdrängende Chinesen haben das Gebiet um einen Teil seiner ursprünglichen Atmosphäre gebracht. Doch eigens von Italienern gegründete Vereine bemühen sich darum, von *Little Italy* zu retten, was noch zu retten ist. Viele Restaurants, Pizzerias und Cafés sind hier bis heute noch ganz und gar italienisch geprägt, und ein Höhepunkt italienischen Lebensstils ist das San-Gennaro-Fest im September, wenn Italiener in Tracht und bunte Karren zu Ehren des hl. Januarius, des Schutzpatrons von Neapel wie von Little Italy, durch die Hauptstraßen ziehen.

Little Italy is one of New York's smallest ethnic quarters. It has lost much of its identity owing to the northward march of Chinatown in recent years, and there are several associations anxious to preserve its original character. The present population, however, is primarily composed of older Italo-Americans, as the young prefer to shift to the outskirts of town. Restaurants, pizzerias and Italian style cafés abound none the less, while on San Gennaro's Day the main streets are crowded with people in traditional costumes and lines of floats commemorate the patron saint of Naples and Little Italy.

96.

97.

«New York ist eine vertikale Stadt, die das Zeichen einer neuen Epoche in sich trägt. Es ist eine Katastrophe, die ein allzu ungestümes Schicksal sich zu eigen gemacht hat, um couragierte, vertrauensvolle Menschen zu überwältigen, auch wenn es sich um eine prachtvolle, großartige Katastrophe handelt».
(Le Corbusier, aus: *«Als die Kathedralen weiß waren»*)

Die Wolkenkratzer drängen sich an den Straßen zusammen, die unaufhörlich von Menschen und Autos wimmeln. Der Mensch wird von dieser Höhe, diesem Reichtum, diesem gleißenden Licht unterdrückt, wird - winzig, wie er ist - in diesen tiefen Schluchten aus Stein, Stahl und Glas erstickt. Aber man darf nicht vergessen, dass gerade dieser winzig kleine Mensch all dies mit seinem Geist, seinem Herzen und seinen Händen geschaffen hat.

«New York is a vertical city bearing the brand of a new epoch. A catastrophe that an over-violent fate has used to overwhelm, a courageous, confident people. A magnificent, grandiose catastrophe, none the less».
(Le Corbusier, *When cathedrals were white*).

Life among the skyscrapers that pack the steets is a constant swarming of people and vehicles. Oppressed by height, wealth and dazzling lights, a single human being is but a tiny creature drowned in these deep valleys of stone, steel and glass. A moment's thought, however, reminds us that all this is the work of men's minds, hands and hearts.

98.

Brooklyn, einer der fünf Distrikte von New York City, ist die größte Stadt der Vereinigten Staaten, die in einer anderen Stadt aufgegangen ist. Sie war im Jahr 1636 von holländischen Einwanderern gegründet und nach einer kleinen holländischen Stadt auf den Namen *Breuckelen* getauft worden, und bis zum 1898 erfolgten Anschluss an New York City blieb sie eine unabhängige Stadt mit eigener Kommunalverwaltung. Der im westlichen Teil von *Long Island* gelegene Distrikt wird oft auch als *«Rooming House»* bezeichnet, als «Schlafsaal»; denn viele seiner Einwohner arbeiten in Manhattan, das sie mühelos mit U-Bahn, Bahn, Fährschiffen, Autos und Bussen erreichen können. Drei Brücken verbinden *Brooklyn* mit Manhattan, darunter auch die *Brooklyn Bridge* (Foto 75), die bei ihrer Einweihung als achtes Weltwunder bezeichnet wurde. In *Brooklyn* sind viele Industriebetriebe zu Hause, es besitzt eine der größten Werften der Welt, und von seinen Hafendocks legen Frachtschiffe ab, die die unterschiedlichsten Waren in alle Kontinente der Welt bringen.

Brooklyn is one of New York's five boroughs and the largest city within a city in the United States. Founded as Breuckelen (after a small town near Utrecht) by Dutch settlers in 1636, it grew into an independent city and was not merged with New York until 1898. Situated in the western part of Long Island, Brooklyn is often called «The Rooming House», since so many of its residents travel by subway, railway, ferryboats, buses and cars to work in Manhattan. Three bridges, in fact, cross the East River. Brooklyn Bridge (photo 75) was once regarded as the eighth wonder of the world, since it is an early example of suspension construction. Brooklyn has many factories and a large dockland where freighters are loaded with merchandise of every kind for transport around the world.

99.

100.

Der *South Street Seaport* war einst die wichtigste Zugangspforte zu New York. In diesem südlich der *Brooklyn Bridge* am *East River* gelegenen Hafen erwuchs der Überseehandel, der mit zur Entwicklung der Stadt beigetragen hat. Als die Segelschiffe um 1860 durch Dampfschiffe ersetzt wurden, musste der größte Teil der Hafentätigkeit an den *Hudson River* verlegt werden, wo mehr Platz für immer mächtigere Piers vorhanden war. Die Gegend am *East River* verlor daher an Bedeutung und verfiel, und erst im Jahr 1967 begannen am ehemaligen Hafen und in dessen Umgebung Sanierungsarbeiten, und es wurde das *South Street Seaport Museum* gegründet. In den Achtzigerjahren setzte eine Revitalisierungsaktion des gesamten Hafenareals ein, das unter Denkmalschutz gestellt wurde. An den Kais liegen alte Schiffe, die einst zwischen Europa und Amerika verkehrten und auch im Inneren besichtigt werden können.

The South Street Seaport was once New York's main point of entry. Situated on the East River south of the Brooklyn Bridge, it received the sailing vessels whose trade swelled the city's importance. When sail began to give way to steam at the end of the 1860s, however, there was a general move to the deeper anchorages in the Hudson River, where there was also plenty of room for longer and wider piers, and the area quickly declined. Rehabilitation of the port began in 1967 with the establishment of the South Street Seaport Museum, while in the Eighties the area was declared of historical interest and its full-scale restoration was begun. Some historic vessels of the type that used to ply between Europe and America are tied up at two of the piers.

101.

Auf den Plätzen und Straßen New Yorks sind neben traditionellen Denkmälern auch viele moderne Skulpturen anzutreffen. Beispielhaft ist der sieben Meter hohe «Cube» von Isamu Noguchi, der im Jahr 1973 im Financial District, vor dem Gebäude Nr. 140 am Broadway, aufgestellt wurde.

Numerous modern sculptures can be seen in New York's streets and squares as well as conventional monuments. One example is the 21-ft high «Cube» designed by Isamu Noguchi in 1973 and located in front of No. 140 Broadway in the Financial District.

102.

Auf der *South Street* und den anderen Straßen und Plätzen des Hafenviertels finden im Frühjahr und im Sommer Ausstellungen im Freien statt, die thematisch zur Hafengegend passen. Die Fassade des Hauses Nr. 41 der *Peck Slip* ist von Richard Haas mit einem großen Trompe-l'œil ausgeschmückt worden: die optische Täuschung einer von Häusern und Geschäften gesäumten Straße, die sich gegen die *Brooklyn Bridge* im Hintergrund öffnet.

Shows and exhibitions in keeping with the nature of the port area are held in spring and summer along South Street and the adjoining side roads and squares. A fascinating *trompe-l'œil* painted by Richard Haas on the wall of a house in one of these roads (No. 41, Peck Slip) depicts a street with houses and shops, and the Brooklyn Bridge in the background.

103.

104.

New York, diese einzigartige, außergewöhnliche Stadt, kann die unterschiedlichsten, gegensätzlichsten Emotionen hervorrufen. Es ist alles und das Gegenteil von allem. Seine Größe überwältigt, überrascht und erdrückt. Das zu Große und das zu Kleine, das Erhabene und das Klägliche sind hier die ständigen Begleiter. Es ist schwer, ein objektives Urteil über die Stadt abzugeben. *Goodbye New York*. Dein protziger Reichtum und deine Armut, deine nach Opulenz riechenden Wolkenkratzer, deine berühmten Theater, deine gedrängt vollen Straßen, deine riesigen oder heimeligen Parks, deine berühmten Universitäten, deine Museen, deine Farben, deine Ghettos, die weiße, gelbe, schwarze Hautfarbe deiner Einwohner - all dies verflicht sich zu einem einzigen, lebendigen Eindruck: Du bist die Kathedrale des Menschen und seines Geistes, seiner Arbeit und seines Wahnsinns.

New York is an extraordinary city, *sui generis,* the source of conflicting feelings, since it is both everything and its opposite. Its grandeur impresses, surprises and suffocates. The over-great and the over-small, magnificence and meanness are one's constant companions. A balanced judgement is out of the question. Goodbye New York. Ostentatious wealth and poverty, skyscrapers oozing opulence, theatres, crowded streets, immense and tiny parks, universities and museums, ghettos, skins that are black, white and yellow, colours of every kind – what are these but evidence that here is a cathedral of mankind, the expression of its ingenuity, its toil and its folly?